Planning in the moment has transformed both our practice and ourselves here at Gunter. It has taken us from interferers to interactors, privileged to play with the children in our setting. Children are demonstrating far higher levels of interest and involvement, persevering and showing a "can do" attitude whilst creativity, critical thinking and motivation for all is evident in the constant thrum of activity. For the teaching staff, planning, preparation and assessment is now a celebration of children's learning. Inputting the children's "Wow!" moments, contributed by all the staff, is a delight and leads naturally to knowing what's next. The change has given us the freedom to teach in accordance with children's needs and in a way that is nourishing for them and us.

Chris Dingley, Early Years Lead, Gunter Primary School, Birmingham, UK

We began putting planning in the moment into action in September 2016 after some considerable time getting our environment right. At the end of our first year I can see how it has benefitted both staff and the children in our care. The staff are now much less stressed, more relaxed and are free to spend quality time with the children, ensuring that no teachable moment is missed. They have all commented on how much better they feel they know their key children. The children's personal, emotional and social development has surpassed that of previous cohorts. They are much more resilient, independent and show an excitement for learning, safe in the knowledge that the adults will follow their lead.

Nikki Smith, Manager, Little Learners Pre-school, Waltham Cross, UK

Having used "in the moment" planning all year we have seen fantastic results. The children have amazed us with their independence, desire to learn and ability to reflect on their own learning. Our GLD is the highest it has ever been but, more importantly, the children are happy, engaged and truly involved and excited by their own learning. Our journey to fully implement "in the moment" planning has been wondrous. I can't thank Anna enough for giving us the confidence to teach in a way we love. It has been a leap of faith for everyone but has been totally worth it and I would recommend it to anyone.

Suzi Strutt, Early Years Team Leader and Reception Teacher,
Thorley Hill Primary School, Bishop's Stortford, UK

Planning in the Moment with Young Children

Young children live in the here and now. If adults are to make a real difference to their learning they need to seize the moments when children first show curiosity, and support their next steps immediately. This book embraces the concept of planning "in the moment" and emphasises the critical role of the adult in promoting child-led learning, giving early years practitioners the confidence and insight to work and plan in the moment, and enabling the children in their care to live, learn, play and develop in the here and now.

Planning in the Moment with Young Children maintains a strong link to practice, providing numerous examples of how practitioners can integrate spontaneous planning and rich adult–child interactions into their everyday practice and early years curricula. From time-tabling to setting clear rules, creating enabling environments, keeping records and making use of a variety of materials, the book demonstrates the multitude of ways in which practitioners can encourage child autonomy and respond to the unique needs of each child. Examples from practice are rooted in theory, fully contextualised, and exemplified by original documentation sourced from the author's own experiences and from a wide variety of settings.

Key features include:

- over 180 full-colour photographs to illustrate practice;
- photocopiable pages including planning sheets, documentation and activity sheets;
- advice on working with parents, individual children and groups;
- tailored guidance on working with children at different stages of development from birth to age 6 years;
- relevance to a range of settings, including childminders, pre-schools, nurseries and schools.

When children are allowed to select where, with what, and how to play, they are truly invested in their play, they become deeply involved and make dramatic progress. This book is an outstanding testament to a responsive and child-led way of working in early years environments. Practitioners will be guided, inspired and supported to work spontaneously and reactively – planning as they go and celebrating the results!

Anna Ephgrave has been teaching for over 27 years. Her most recent post was Assistant Head Teacher responsible for the early years and year one at Carterhatch Infant School, which was graded as Outstanding in its most recent inspection. Anna is now an independent consultant, trainer and author, supporting practitioners both in the United Kingdom and abroad. She has written three very successful books for David Fulton, Routledge: *The Reception Year in Action*, *Year One in Action*, and *The Nursery Year in Action*, which was the winner of Nursery World's Professional Books Award, 2017.

Planning in the Moment with Young Children

A Practical Guide for Early Years Practitioners and Parents

Anna Ephgrave

Routledge
Taylor & Francis Group

LONDON AND NEW YORK

First published 2018
by Routledge
2 Park Square, Milton Park, Abingdon, Oxon OX14 4RN

and by Routledge
711 Third Avenue, New York, NY 10017

Routledge is an imprint of the Taylor & Francis Group, an informa business

British Library Cataloguing in Publication Data
A catalogue record for this book is available from the British Library

Library of Congress Cataloging in Publication Data
A catalog record for this book has been requested

ISBN: 978-1-138-08036-2 (hbk)
ISBN: 978-1-138-08039-3 (pbk)
ISBN: 978-1-315-11350-0 (ebk)

Typeset in Univers
by Keystroke, Neville Lodge, Tettenhall, Wolverhampton

Contents

6 Assessment and record-keeping **131**

Assessments and evidence – practitioner's knowledge 131

Conclusion **139**

Acknowledgements

This book should have taken a couple of months to complete, but it has actually taken nearly a year. This is partly due to the mesmerising distraction that is my new granddaughter and partly due to the complexity of the topic. However, it is also due to the fact that I wanted to include examples and information from a variety of settings, a mixture of practitioners and a range of children from birth to age six. I approached various people whom I have worked with in recent years to ask for contributions, and I have been overwhelmed by the response and generosity from everyone. I received hundreds of photographs, testimonials, samples of planning sheets and messages of support. I then had the delightful task of reading everything and looking at the lovely images in order to weave as much as possible into the text. The result, I believe, has been worth the extra time and I hope readers will agree. Therefore, I would like to thank the children, parents and staff in the following settings, for their contributions, without which this book would not have been as vibrant and varied.

- Brindishe Green Primary School, Lewisham, London
- British School, Muscat, Oman
- Caldecote Primary School, Leicester
- Caversham Nursery School, Reading
- Chichester Nursery School, Chichester
- Childminder (anonymous), Blackpool
- Clare Peck, parent, teacher and member of Keeping Early Years Unique
- Gunter Primary School, Birmingham
- Henry Bradley Infant School, Chesterfield, Derbyshire
- Little Explorers, Thornton, Lancashire
- Little Learners Pre-school, Cheshunt, Hertfordshire
- Oasis Academy Hobmoor, Birmingham
- Richmond Avenue Primary School, Southend-On-Sea, Essex
- Staple Hill Stars Pre-school, Bristol
- St Mary's Primary School, Whitstable, Kent
- The Nest Nurseries, Birmingham
- Thorley Hill Primary School, Bishop's Stortford, Hertfordshire

Finally, I would like to give a special mention to Amy Claypole and her sister Olivia Langham from Daffodils Outdoor Nursery, Market Harborough, Leicestershire. Olivia is a practitioner and a photographer, putting her in the unique position of being able to take candid shots of children in the setting. Like the nursery itself, the images are beautiful and I cannot thank everyone enough for their generosity in sharing these photographs.

Introduction

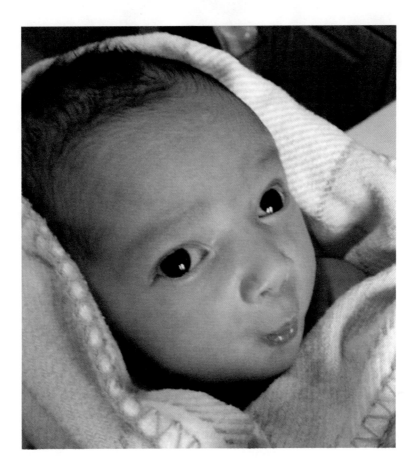

Planning in the moment is nothing new. It is exactly what a responsive parent does with their child every day. It is exactly what skilful practitioners have always done. Every time an adult looks at, and listens to, a child, they are assessing and "planning" how to respond. These assessments and plans are based on the adult's observations of the child in that moment and also draw on any previous knowledge of the child. The response is "planned" **in the moment** and is uniquely suited to that unique child in that unique moment. The adult will be considering (either consciously or instinctively) whether they can add anything in that moment to benefit the child. If so, they will respond and interact accordingly, supporting the child to develop.

In the past ten years, I have been developing some simple paperwork on which **a small proportion** of these adult–child interactions can be recorded (after the event). Again, the format of this paperwork is nothing new – it is basically blank sheets of paper. I will state here, and this influences the whole book, that the paperwork has minimal impact on the children and is therefore not as important as the interactions themselves. In many settings, there is an obsession with evidencing and recording everything, and this must be addressed. Practitioners need to get back to the important, powerful role of interacting with children, rather than trying to document everything that happens. By doing so, they will regain a love of their job and the children will make outstanding progress – a "win–win" situation. This book aims to explain what this might look like in a variety of settings and with children at varying stages of development. My hope is that it will support practitioners to feel confident in focusing on the important aspect of their role – observing and interacting with children as they play.

So – put your clipboards down, put your electronic tablets away, forget any pre-conceived activity plans or learning objectives. Open the doors and play with the children – plan as you go, plan on the hoof, plan spontaneously, plan responsively – call it what you like. The important thing is that **you are led by the child in the moment and you respond accordingly**.

From birth to . . .

As I write this introduction, my granddaughter is just four weeks old. My daughter has been planning in the moment for the past four weeks. She is constantly alert to her baby's needs – watching, listening and responding – twenty-four hours a day. She can distinguish between the various cries and knows when the baby is hungry, tired, alert, uncomfortable or in pain. She then decides whether to feed her, sing to her, walk her round the garden, change her nappy or rub her back. There is no "plan" for each day, other than to look after her baby. She does this by observing her closely and responding accordingly.

It is already obvious that this baby is curious and interested in the world around her. She is "hard-wired" to learn. Her brain is growing rapidly at this time – with thousands of new synapses forming each second. While her needs are being met, she is content. Any anxiety, pain, discomfort or need is met by her responsive parents. She is learning that people are there to care for her and she is beginning to respond to them too. She is staring intently at faces, turning her head to the sound of voices, experimenting with her own voice and settling when sung to – totally captivating. Soon she will smile. This innate desire to develop will continue throughout her life but she is unique and will thrive if the adults around her recognise this uniqueness and respond to her accordingly.

It is the same for every baby and child in the world. They are each born with this desire to learn and to be part of a social world and it is our responsibility to cater to each child as a unique individual, rather than as a name on a register or, worse, a piece of data. Whenever adults try to force a child to do something which they do not want to do, they cause the child anxiety which changes the chemical make-up of the brain and prevents new synapse formation. This is true for all – not just babies. Therefore, it is absolutely critical that we **start with the child**, be led by the child and find ways to respond which suit the child.

In this way, the child will remain content and new learning is possible. Thus, progress will be maximised by constantly protecting the well-being of a child (ensuring they feel secure, valued and understood) and then responding to them in ways that respect and value their unique identity.

Babies, young children and older children thrive when treated in this responsive, respectful way. A child who loves to be outdoors, on the move and chatting to himself will find it very stressful to sit still indoors, in silence. This stress will inhibit new learning. Far better to allow this child to be outdoors, learning in an active way. A child who likes quiet and calm, producing intricate models with the tiniest of construction pieces, will thrive indoors with space and time to bring his/her ideas to fruition. These children are different – one is not "better" than the other – and, as practitioners, we need to find a way to cater to each child, rather than trying to force children to fit into a particular model or style of learning. The ideas presented in this book will, hopefully, support practitioners in achieving this.

    But what about test results? I am only too aware of the relentless pressure placed on teachers in schools to achieve "results" and indeed for all practitioners to deliver good, or better, progress. Lead practitioners, whether owners, managers, childminders or head teachers, are all accountable for the progress of the children in their settings. However, those who understand child development and understand how children learn, will know that if we can find ways to treat each child in a unique way, then the results will be the best possible. It is a leap of faith to trust that the innate desire to learn, recognised in babies, is ever present. This desire exists throughout a child's life and therefore the ideas presented in this book can be applied to children of all ages. In my 27-year career, I have seen the success that can be achieved through child-led learning with children of all ages. When a child has autonomy and independence, supported by an enabling environment and skilful adults, then they make superb progress. Once the progress is demonstrated, then practitioners, including head teachers, are able to defend and develop this practice further. This book might help some of those leaders take that initial leap, see the results and then continue to tap into the powerful potential of child-led learning.

This is a journey and practitioners, who are contemplating change in their practice, need a clear plan for their journey of change. This book is organised in a way that supports this. It starts by explaining how children learn best, which must be the guiding factor in any setting. Once practitioners are clear about how children learn, they can then assess everything that they do in terms of whether it supports this or not. The book then goes on to look at all such practicalities – routines, expectations, environments, interactions, record-keeping and assessment – constantly reflecting on whether they support the best outcomes for children. Thus the journey of change can be completed by tackling each area of practice as described in the book: understand **why** child-initiated play is so powerful, then tackle **how** it can be organised, be clear that skilful adults are constantly **planning in the moment** and finally **celebrate the results**.

ACTION PLAN

Have a team discussion to find out how practitioners are feeling about their setting. What is going well? What is causing stress? What is most beneficial to the children?

Write a paragraph that describes how your setting is run now and a summary of the feelings of the staff.

Our EYFS and Y1 team were incredibly inspired after receiving INSET focused on planning and teaching in the moment. Y1 had previously been quite formal, particularly towards the end of the year. But within a few days the four class unit had been transformed. Although each class still has their own classroom and class teacher, each room, outdoor space and corridor becomes an exciting "workshop" during "free flow" when all of the children are able to choose when, where and how their learning takes place. Also, as the whole unit is opened up to every child, each can choose who they work with which has supported the development of social skills tremendously. Despite not having topics, and planning being based on the children's interests, we have found that, through spending time ensuring that the environment and adult support matches the learning needs, we have covered the National Curriculum and more! Children are much more engaged in their learning and now take their own learning journey very seriously and can articulate their next steps very well. *Story Scribing* has been amazingly successful, particularly with our boys. The Focus child meetings with parents have been so successful that we have introduced that system throughout the whole school, doing away with formal parents' evenings. The response from staff, parents but, most of all, the children, has been extremely positive. In our recent Inspection the provision and results in Year 1 came out as one of our major strengths. We are now planning to introduce many of the elements into Year 2 next year and KS2 teachers are champing at the bit!

Hillary Hinchliff, Head of Primary, British School Muscat, Oman, **2017**

The matter is very different when our methods and conditions are better adapted to the child's normal modes of growth and spontaneous interests. If the child has ample opportunity for free play and bodily exercise, if his love of making and doing with his hands is met, if his intelligent interest in the world around him is encouraged by sympathy and understanding, if he is left free to make-believe or to think as his impulses take him, then his advances in skill and understanding are but welcome signs of mental health and vigour.

Susan Isaacs, *The Nursery Years*, Routledge & Kegan Paul, London, **1929**

Staple Hill Stars Preschool, Bristol

1 | Brain development

The vision

If you visited a "utopian" setting, what would you notice about the children?

This is one of the first questions that I ask any group of practitioners – be they parents, childminders, pre-school staff, nursery nurses, teachers or headteachers. It applies whether the children are four months old or 18 years old. The answer is always the same. The first thing indicating that a setting is working is that **the children are ENGAGED.** Throughout this book, whenever the word "engaged" is used, it refers to **Level 5 involvement** as described by Ferre Laevers – see Appendix A. Many other words are then listed – the children are happy, independent, confident, unique, taking risks, taking the lead, communicating, challenged, creative, secure, curious, persistent, sociable, enthusiastic, empathic and so on.

However, it soon becomes clear that engagement is the key indicator. For example, a child who is not happy cannot become deeply engaged. A child who is not challenged by what is on offer will not be engaged. A child who is being controlled by adults will not be as deeply engaged. A child who feels insecure (for whatever reason) will not be able to become deeply engaged.

We know intuitively that our vision is to get all children **engaged.** Our intuition is justified and now we need to articulate the underlying rationale for this belief: **When children are deeply engaged, their brain is developing and new synapses are forming – i.e. they are making progress.**

We also know that a child who is bored, passive, quiet and not engaged is not making progress – their brain is not growing when in that state. We do not need to carry out an

experiment to prove this. Brain scans clearly demonstrate this and the long-term effects of low engagement have been demonstrated in the case of the Romanian orphans born during the 1970s and 1980s. Although **these children were able to learn to read and write at a later stage in their lives**, their ability to empathise and form relationships has proved almost impossible. There are two main points to conclude from this; that lack of engagement hinders brain development, and also the need to focus on social skills and empathy at a young age because this is very difficult to develop later.

We must also recognise and believe that every child wants to be engaged. If we have children who are not engaged, we cannot blame them. We must look to see what we can do to engage them. The work of Professor Ferre Laevers is complimented by the work of Bowlby and supports the approach and beliefs that I observe in practitioners all over the world. This can be presented in various ways but, in simple terms, babies need to form trusting relationships at a young age. This then allows them to be in a "secure" state, in which their natural desire to learn and develop can be optimised. Anything which disrupts this state will alter the chemical make-up in the brain and hinder development. Thus, the developmentally inappropriate practice of formalised, adult-led learning that is being imposed on so many young children is actually preventing the very development that these practices are supposed to promote.

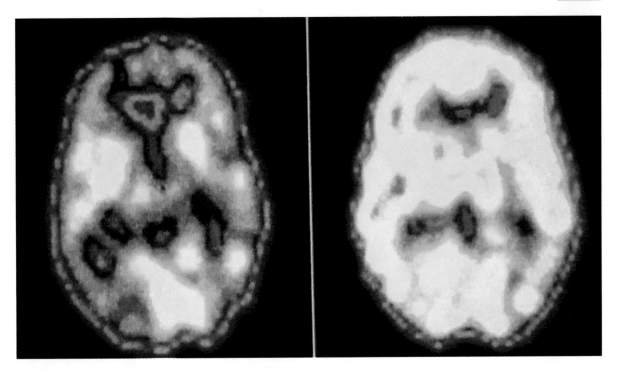

Not engaged – Level 1 involvement   Engaged – Level 5 involvement

Levels of involvement

Ferre Laevers developed descriptors for various levels of involvement and these can be used as a simple, objective way of measuring the engagement of an individual, group or class. The descriptors are given in Appendix A. I have often shown these to external inspectors and their response is that the Level 5 (with concentration, creativity, energy and persistence) is equivalent to an "outstanding" grade.

There are many ways in which these levels of involvement can be used, as outlined below.

Individual children

As mentioned above, we start with the assumption that all children want to be engaged, i.e. they want to be at Level 5. In a superb setting, if a child is not becoming engaged, then the descriptors can be used to monitor a child at regular intervals throughout a day or a week in order to uncover patterns or preferences. Always bear in mind with such a child that there might be external factors causing emotional well-being to be affected, and remember that a child with poor emotional well-being is not able to become deeply engaged. However, such monitoring can be a powerful way to see which sessions or events do engage a child and which clearly do not. Starting with the assumption that they do want to be engaged, it is then possible to see which types of session are "working" for the particular child.

Groups or class

The same descriptors can be used to consider group or whole class sessions. Again, assuming that we are aiming to deliver practice that will see most children at Level 4 or 5, we can quickly start to see which sessions or events are appropriate and productive, in terms of engagement/involvement (and, therefore, progress). For example, if we are delivering an input on the carpet, then we should have the level descriptors in mind. When the children start to fidget and become distracted, then this tells us that the session has become unproductive. It does not tell us that the children are "naughty" or that "they can't concentrate" or that "they have ADHD". It tells us that what we are offering is not engaging and therefore is not supporting synapse formation and learning. Once we accept this, it is clear that group sessions for babies are rarely appropriate. Equally, carpet sessions that are longer than a few minutes are not appropriate for three year olds. Assembly for Reception children is not going to deliver engagement and nor are lengthy phonic sessions for a child at any age. I would also urge practitioners to use these levels to measure the effectiveness of focussed tasks, snack time, circle time and so on. In all these cases, the level of involvement is often very low, the adults and children can become quite stressed and the learning is minimal. It is, then, a very useful tool for practitioners to use as a way of assessing practice and then arguing for change.

Environment

The levels can also be used to see which areas of an environment are "working" – which areas are delivering good levels of involvement and which are not. This is an ongoing process, particularly with some age groups, as their interests and stage of development can change dramatically over the course of a few months. However, some areas are always engaging and others rarely so. Also, the levels of involvement will help practitioners see which areas are rarely, if ever, used. Such areas obviously need to be changed as they are essentially "wasted space". Chapter 3 on environment gives detailed information and ideas to support the development of an environment that is engaging.

A section of an outdoor area where the levels of involvement were low.

Involvement levels improved dramatically once the area was developed.

Resources

I would recommend using the levels as a way of assessing the effectiveness of resources. Whether or not there is a large budget, it is best to have mainly resources which are open-ended and can therefore be used in many different ways. For example, for small world play, rather than having a pirate ship, a doll's house, a castle, a rocket, a caravan, a farm and a car park for the children to use, there is far more potential for engagement with wooden blocks, Lego, pieces of fabric, paper and pens etc. In this way, the children can create their own rocket, car park, castle and so on. Again, further details can be found in Chapter 3.

Child-initiated play – autonomy and genuine choice

So how do we achieve the best levels of involvement? I have worked with children since the age of 13. I grew up in the Woodcraft Folk and, at 13 years old, was organising a group for six to ten year olds. This voluntary work continued for over 30 years. I also had a baby while studying at university and a second baby a couple of years later. When my children were very young, I worked as a child-minder and also ran toddler groups in the local area. I became a teacher 27 years ago and was also a foster carer for ten years whilst teaching. I have experience of children of many ages and in many different situations. I have also read and studied, not only for qualifications, but also out of fascination and, sometimes, frustration when trying to find the best ways in which to support young children. Everything in my life experiences – personal, voluntary, professional and academic – has led me to conclude that, once they feel secure, **children become most deeply engaged when they have autonomy**, when they are able to choose what to do.

What is more, nothing in my life has ever demonstrated that this is not true. This applies to a newborn baby, a toddler, a vulnerable foster child, a child on the autistic spectrum, a child who speaks no English, a Year One child, a child with a "gifted" label or a child with additional needs.

To summarise, the best levels of involvement – leading to the best progress – are achieved when children's well-being is high and we then let them choose what to do. This has become known as "free-flow play", "child-initiated play", "choosing time", "explore and learn time", "continuous provision", etc. But, to be clear – within agreed boundaries – I am talking about children **playing** where they want, with whatever they choose, for as long as they want, in whatever way they want.

This sounds simple but, if every child in a setting is to be able to play as they choose, there are several things that need to be in place in order to support this:

- A prioritisation of well-being above all else, recognising that high well-being is critical in order for a child to feel secure, which in turn will allow them to become involved.
- Consistent boundaries, expectations and routines (within which each child can then relax and have the freedom that they need in order to learn effectively).
- An enabling environment (which is organised to meet the ever-changing needs and interests of each unique child). This book will be of interest to people working from home and also in various settings. Therefore, the words "room", "class", "setting" etc. should be read as meaning the "space" where the children are.
- Skilful, empathic adults interacting appropriately to form warm relationships and to support each child in a way that respects them, preserves their autonomy and offers genuine interest and fascination. Throughout this book, I use the words "adult", "practitioner", "teacher", but these all refer to any adult who is responsible for a child.
- Manageable systems of assessment and record-keeping (to satisfy any statutory requirements, without impeding the progress of the children, and while maintaining the sanity of the staff).

These things are dealt with in the following chapters and each is critical if the **play** is to be successful and productive. What is **not necessary** are any written forward plans. If the children have genuine choice, if it is genuinely child-initiated play, then **we do not know what the children will choose** to do and **we cannot, therefore, pre-plan the activities or the learning outcomes**.

ACTION PLAN

Hold a staff meeting and agree a **vision**.

Ask staff how they want the children to be. (A powerful vision is to aim to have children who are ENGAGED and HAPPY.)

Clarify that "ENGAGED" means Level 5 involvement.

Once the children were free to have the time to really follow their own interests, to really have the time to become deeply involved, and staff had the freedom and time to play with the children, then we realised the true potential of these little people. The children's learning is deeply ingrained. Everything they do is for a real reason. This year, one of my boys wrote our Christmas play! Our girls design woodwork models, they write letters, songs, notices, plans, invitations and story after story. . . . No child thinks that they cannot write. In fact, they write profusely, for every reason imaginable. Their numeracy skills are built up through practical investigations and application. The children constantly display high levels of involvement and well-being and they practically apply the Characteristics of Effective Learning.

Angela Thorogood, Early Years Team Leader, St Mary's Primary School, Whitstable, Kent, **2017**

The Nursery School has embraced "in the moment" planning and, despite the reservations of some staff at the beginning, all are fully signed up to it now. Our data this year, which we have of course been watching very carefully, shows that our boys have made amazing progress over the last year and outstripped their level of development (on or above developmental expectation) scores in every curriculum area and every strand of learning, compared to last year!

Jenny Buckley, Headteacher, Chichester Nursery School, **2017**

The child should postpone reading until 8 or 9 years old, on the grounds that social and sensuous education – doing, moving, seeing, adapting to friends – is interrupted if book study begins too soon.

Dora Russell, *In Defence of Children*, Hamish Hamilton, London, **1932**

Staple Hill Stars Preschool, Bristol

2 Relationships and routines

I am often asked if I will deliver training around behaviour and my answer is no. In settings where all the children are deeply involved in their chosen play, then experience has shown that there will be very few behaviour issues. Training must start by looking at the practice and assessing this by looking at the levels of involvement. **Once the practice improves, the involvement improves and the behaviour improves.** We must start with the assumption that children want to be involved, ensure that this is possible in the practice on offer, and then tackle any behaviour issues that remain.

Trusting relationships, transitions and induction

If a child has low level well-being, they will not be able to engage, no matter how superb the setting is. Well-being is built on a foundation of trusting relationships. It is beyond the scope of this book to examine all the possible situations that could mean that a child has not built up trusting relationships from birth. However, practitioners should keep in mind that without good well-being, a child cannot become engaged and deeply involved in learning. No matter how wonderful a home has been, a young child still needs time

and empathy to build relationships with the new adults they encounter (in a setting) and to understand the new routines and expectations. Transitions and induction are therefore critical.

When a child sets off for their first day at a new setting, they should be full of positive emotions – excitement, confidence and happiness. This happens if the child knows exactly where they are going, who will be there, what they will be able to do on arrival and how long they will be staying there. A successful transition means that the child settles quickly – meaning that they have good emotional well-being and can therefore relax and play immediately – thus learning and developing from day one. Practitioners then greet happy children (whom they already know very well) and these children are settled, confident and thus able to learn.

In the worst case of transition, in Reception for example, 30 children arrive at 9 a.m. on the first day of term, to a school they have never visited, met by staff they do not know and where their parents are not allowed to stay with them. "Barbaric" is the word that comes to mind, but unfortunately this situation does still happen.

This book covers a large age range and a variety of settings, but transition procedures are absolutely critical. It is during this period that practitioners can start to build a relationship with the child and the family. Some ideas are as follows (again, as appropriate for the age group being worked with):

- Visit the setting that the child is currently attending.
- Organise play sessions/visits at your setting (for parent and child).
- Home visit each family and get a family photo.
- Use all information to inform the organisation of your environment.
- Plan the induction period meticulously (see below).

The **induction/settling period** is critical, must be planned carefully and should take as long as is needed for the child to feel secure and relaxed. The main message is to invest as much time as necessary in the settling period and involve parents as much as possible in order to "teach" their own child how to "be" in the setting. Parents can even be given a "prompt" card with a list of things to do with their child while they are settling them (**as appropriate for the child's age**). For example:

- Remind your child about the lovely adults in the setting (and their names).
- Show your child how to self-register.
- Teach your child how to take off their coat and hang it on their peg.
- Show your child the toilets and make sure they can use them independently (if appropriate).
- Show your child around the setting and explain that they can play indoors or outside.
- Explain to your child that they can play with anything but when they have finished, the things must be put away.
- Play with your child and show them how to use the resources.
- Ensure that your child walks indoors and uses a quiet voice indoors.

Some parents find it reassuring to have little tasks such as this to do. It is also a good opportunity to observe how parents interact with their children.

If the practice is superb and a child is still not becoming engaged, then this usually means that there is an **issue with well-being**, possibly related to events at home or in the past. The child might have attachment disorder, be suffering from the effects of trauma or be living in a volatile home situation. As stated above, it is beyond the scope of this book to go into detail about the numerous situations which might lead to poor well-being. However, it is our responsibility to ensure that it is not the practice that is preventing the engagement so that we can then seek external support and plan how to address issues that are outside of the setting.

The aim should be that, by the time a child is left by the parent, staff already have a relationship with the child, and their family, and the child is already familiar with the setting. When successful, most children then settle immediately when the parents eventually leave. Some children (whatever age) may need a parent with them for several weeks and staff should accommodate this for as long as necessary (even in Reception classes). Sometimes, after a few sessions, I would encourage a parent to stay in the room, but to just sit and read. This allows the child to relax in the knowledge that their parent is nearby. The child is then more likely to have a positive experience and will want to be there even if their parent is not. The most important aspect of the decision about when a parent can leave is that it is made jointly with the parents and that the child is aware of what is happening.

Key person systems

For younger children and babies, the practitioner who carries out the home visit, and who spends time settling a new child, should be the key person for that child. However, the subject of the key person role has become very confused in many settings.

The Early Years Foundation Stage (EYFS) statutory guidance states that:

> Each child must be assigned a key person. Providers must inform parents and/or carers of the name of the key person, and explain their role, when a child starts attending a setting. The key person must help ensure that every child's learning and care is tailored to meet their individual needs. The key person must seek to engage and support parents and/or carers in guiding their child's development at home. They should also help families engage with more specialist support if appropriate.
>
> EYFS, p. 10, § 1.10

The same EYFS document states that in a Reception class the legal requirement for adult–child ratios is 1:30. Therefore, in a class where there are 30 children and one teacher, then that teacher becomes the key person for every child. In many schools, even where there are two or three adults in a Reception class, the school makes the decision that the teacher will be the key person for all the children (in nursery and Reception). This decision complies with the requirements of the law and is also appropriate for Reception-age children. But there is still great confusion around this issue in many settings.

Although there is a legal requirement for each child to have a key person, there is no stipulation about how a setting should organise this. For younger children and babies in nurseries and children's centres, it is vital that they have a familiar key person with whom they can form an attachment. Indeed, advances in the understanding of attachment theory and attachment disorders underpin this piece of legislation. In brief, a baby who receives responsive care and attention from their main carer, will develop a good attachment and relationship to that carer. As they grow older, they will be able to form successful relationships with others. Conversely, if a baby receives inadequate or inconsistent care and attention they can develop an attachment disorder, and one of the main outcomes of this is an inability to form relationships as they grow older.

Obviously the practitioner is a young baby's main carer if the baby is in day care from 8 a.m. until 6 p.m., and this needs to be the same person for as much of that time as possible.

However, at nursery and Reception level, most children have developed a strong attachment to a parent and are able to cope with shared attention from a few adults in nursery or school. It is therefore acceptable to say that the teacher (in school nursery and Reception classes) will be the key person for all the children, supported by the other members of staff. If a child or parent forms a trusting working relationship with a particular member of the staff team, they can always talk to that staff member, rather than the teacher, if they wish. If the arrangement has been agreed that the teacher is the key person, then the support staff are still expected to help with any systems of observation, assessment and record-keeping. However, it is ultimately the teacher's responsibility to maintain the paperwork and to take ownership of the class and the progress of ALL the children.

In some schools, it is agreed to allocate groups of children to a different staff member as the key person. Again, this complies with the law. However, it must always be monitored and the amount of responsibility given to support staff should be within their capabilities. The school must also ensure that there is consistency of provision for all children, in terms of their records, observations and assessments. In addition, some schools require the key person to deliver small group sessions on a regular basis. Again, consistency must be assured. It is possible, with such a system, that some children will not receive the same quality of teaching during these group sessions. A more consistent model is to have the teacher as the key person and any group times shared and rotated so that all children receive a consistent quality of teaching.

Chapter 3 explores what the environment needs to be like in order to support the engagement of children. Obviously without a **superb environment**, children will have nothing to do and so will not become engaged and this can lead to behaviour issues with children who are bored and looking for challenges.

If transition is correct, benefits can be reaped for the whole year. Children will be deeply engaged in their learning because they are with adults who know and understand them in an enabling environment that meets their needs and interests. It is definitely worth investing time and energy in this vital aspect of our work.

Timetables and interruptions

Even with good well-being and a superb environment, one of the main aspects of practice that causes stress and tension is the **timetable** and, in particular, **interruptions**. Imagine just starting to read a new novel and being called away to do something else ten minutes later. It would feel annoying and frustrating. Imagine if this happened every time you tried to read the novel. You would soon give up. It is the same for children. The interruption causes them to become annoyed and frustrated, feelings which they might express through their behaviour. In addition, as children get older, if such interruptions occur regularly, they learn that it is not worth investing in their chosen play because they will not be able to see it through to a satisfactory conclusion. When this happens, children start to opt for simpler, less meaningful, play which is easier to leave. This type of play does not deliver Level 5 involvement; that is, it does not involve creativity, concentration, energy or persistence. Rather it is mundane and routine – play that can be left at any moment.

My plea, therefore, is that any interruptions imposed on children's play are considered very carefully and questioned as to their necessity. Any interruptions that cannot be avoided should be moved to the beginning or end of the day or session.

For example, in a room for two year olds, and in many pre-school settings, the children might be stopped for a welcome song, key group time, snack time, focussed tasks and circle time. Each interruption causes the children to stop what they are doing (and this is often play in which they are demonstrating great concentration) and move to a different area of the setting. Moving several two year olds at any one time is very stressful for staff and very frustrating for children – so why do this? Each key person can greet the children as they arrive, they can play alongside them in their chosen play, snacks can be available for the children to have when they want them and focussed tasks and circle time can be removed altogether as they are developmentally not appropriate for such young children. Two year olds want to move around and then collapse for a rest. Then they want to move around again. If this natural cycle is allowed to happen for each child, then stress, frustration and behaviour issues will reduce immediately. Similarly, for three- and four-year-old pre-school children, allow them to play until the end of the session and then have a very short story and song time together before they go home.

This picture shows a very simple visual timetable in a nursery class. There is just one interruption – for "circle time" just before home time.

Another example in which there are numerous interruptions can be seen in many Reception classes (and the interruptions are even more frequent in most Year One classes). I often see timetables such as this:

9.00 a.m.	Whole class registration, welcome, days of the week, etc.
9.15	Assembly
9.30	Whole class literacy input
9.45	"Learn and explore" time indoors, plus focussed activities (45 minutes)
10.30	Whole class snack time
10.45	Play time (in school playground)
11.00	Whole class maths input
11.15	"Learn and explore" time indoors and outside, plus focussed activities (45 minutes)
12.00 p.m.	Phonics
12.30	Lunch
1.30	Whole class Registration and topic input
2.00	"Learn and explore" time indoors and outside, plus focussed activities (45 minutes)
2.45	Tidy up time
3.00	Whole class story time
3.15	Home time

This timetable has numerous transitions and just two hours and 15 minutes of play (some of which is restricted to indoors and some of which will be interrupted when the children are called to do a focussed task).

The timetable in the Reception classes that I work with is as follows:

9.00 a.m.	Self-register. Play – indoors or outside (2 hours and 15 minutes)
11.15	Phonics
11.30	Eat lunch
12.00 p.m.	Play – indoors or outside (2 hours and 50 minutes)
2.50	Tidy up time
3.00	Whole class stories, songs, photos etc.
3.15	Home time

This timetable has just two transitions – one for phonics (and then immediately into lunch) and one for story time (and then immediately home). The children have just over **5 hours of play**.

With fewer interruptions, the levels of involvement increase, and behaviour improves. In addition, for some children, the restriction of staying indoors causes them anxiety and stress. Therefore, if **the doors can be open all day**, this will again improve engagement and behaviour. Many children (and some boys, in particular) are only able to get to Level 5 involvement outdoors and, as there is also 200 per cent more talking outside, so it is beneficial to have the outdoor area available at all times. Indeed, if there are staff shortages at a particular time, why not shut the indoor space?

Another point to note about the second Reception timetable shown above is that **there are no focussed activities**. This means that when the children are playing, the adults are with them, interacting with them and "teaching" them whenever they see an opportunity to do so (see Chapter 4 for further details about this). Once adults are free from focussed tasks, they are available, not only to interact and teach, but also to monitor and scan the setting for any potential behaviour issues. They can then deal with these immediately and appropriately – often taking the time to use such opportunities to **"teach" the children the self-regulation skills** that will support their independence in the future.

For example, if Mira snatches a toy from Ali, an adult will join the pair, give the toy back to Ali and then speak to Mira saying, "If you want that toy, you need to ask Ali – so speak to her and say 'Can I have that toy please?'" The adult will also then speak to Ali and say, "You don't have to give her the toy – you can say 'No, I am using it' or you might say 'You can have it in a minute'." The adult will then encourage the pair to talk like this and resolve the dispute. If a child is upset because another child has shouted at him/her, the adult will again model a response and encourage the child to use it saying, for example, "Don't shout at me. I don't like it." It is not very helpful to say to children "you need to share" or "play nicely" as they do not know what this means. They need specific language such as "You have it for three minutes and then I will have it for three minutes" (using a timer perhaps) or "You have all four trains and I am sad because I have none. Can you give me some?" If the children can come up with solutions for themselves, they are more likely to find a solution the next time without calling on an adult. This level of independence is so valuable and allows the adults to move on to teaching in other areas of development.

It is important to note here that two year olds do not like to share. In an ideal world, they would be at home with a caring parent and, in such a situation, they would not be required to share very often. In this respect, it is very stressful for a two year old to be in a setting with so many other two year olds and this has huge implications on resourcing. In a Reception class, there might be one dustpan and brush and the children will manage to take turns, whereas with children aged two to three, it might be decided to have three dustpans and brushes in order to reduce arguments.

Firm, consistent rules

As stated above, if all children are engaged in play of their own choice, then behaviour issues are often minimal. However, **it is still essential to have firm, consistent rules** within which children can relax and have the freedom to play as they wish. Such rules should be kept to a minimum and should be appropriate to the age of the children in the setting. Every member of the staff team should know what the rules are and should be able to ensure that they are adhered to without the need to raise a voice. A calm, confident, serious tone is often enough to gain compliance. No adult has the right to shout at a young child.

For children aged three or above, a few simple rules might be:

- When we have finished with something, we put it away.
- Indoors, we walk and we use quiet voices.
- No one touches anyone when we are climbing.

Other rules might be added relating to aprons, coats in the rain, and so on, but these need to be agreed with the staff team.

Once the rules are agreed, then everyone has to firmly and calmly ensure that they are followed. For example, if a child drops a book on the floor instead of replacing it on the book rack, then an adult should remind him/her saying, "**First** put the book away and **then** you can go." Once this has been stated, it must be followed through, so "choose your battles". It might take an hour for the child to pick up the book, so make sure you have the time to invest. This is, in fact, exactly what happened to me very recently. Many practitioners worry that this type of event will mean that the children will be unhappy. Actually, the reverse is true. The child in this example was from quite a chaotic home where rules and boundaries were inconsistent and where the children had tantrums to get their own way. This child did eventually pick up the book, I thanked him and he went off to play. The next day, he ran up to me and gave me a hug. He also tidied up happily from then on in the nursery. My ten years as a foster carer taught me that children are testing the boundaries but that they actually want them to remain secure. It is within such boundaries that they can relax, knowing that the adults are in charge and can be trusted (i.e. they mean what they say), and they can then get on with being the child.

It is also preferable to deal with any such behaviour issues immediately and in a way that relates to the behaviour, rather than with reward or sanction charts, etc. In the example above, the child missed out on one hour of playing and therefore decided not to do this again. If a child has scribbled on a table, make sure they clean it off. If a child is running or shouting indoors, then take them outside. If a child is silly with the hammer at the woodwork bench, then they are not allowed to have a turn for a set amount of time. If a child has hurt another child, make sure they look at the other child – an adult can verbalise the feelings of the other child and make sure the child realises how upset you are too. There is little to be gained by making a child say "sorry". It is far more important that they begin to feel some empathy for the child who is hurt and to learn a different way to act next time (using words). So, any consequence should relate to the behaviour.

Also, extrinsic rewards should not play any part in an early years setting. Children are hard-wired to learn, intrinsically motivated to explore and discover, determined to be engaged – they do not need stickers or reward charts for this, they need an enabling environment and skilful staff. A baby who struggles to crawl to reach their favourite toy is rewarded by getting the toy; a child who is trying to master the two-wheeler bike is rewarded by their eventual success – no other reward is needed; a child who has persevered to write a shopping list will be allowed to go to the shops to buy the items listed. Any praise you do give should be around the process, rather than the end result – so praise perseverance, good ideas, initiative, etc. The work around growth mindset is relevant here. It has been shown that children who are told they are "clever" will in fact give up more easily when things get a bit difficult, whereas children who have been praised for perseverance will just keep trying when things get difficult. So **ban the word "clever" from your vocabulary!**

As mentioned in Chapter 1, levels of involvement can be used to assess the value of sessions and, once you start to use this, you will see that **group times often deliver low levels of involvement**. This indicates that they are of little value in terms of brain development, i.e. learning and progress. These sessions often result in children displaying poor behaviour and getting into trouble because they cannot sit still. The simple solution to this behaviour issue is to **stop the group time** – or certainly shorten the length of the session – or make it more interactive and engaging. Whatever you do **you must not blame the children**. If they are not engaged, they are sending you a clear message; they are saying, "This is not how I want to learn. This is not engaging for me. This is a waste of my time." It is very easy to blame the children when, in fact, it is the practice that is inappropriate and needs to be changed.

One other potential cause for lack of engagement is that **young children have not had opportunities to play at home**. Many very young children, and even babies, now spend **several hours in front of screens**, thus lacking opportunities for movement, interaction, speech, empathy and social skills. They can spend hours in isolation, immobile and silent. This can impact on their ability to talk, play, move and socialise. Practitioners need to take this into account during the induction period and beyond. These children will need far longer time spent on these skills. In particular, they will need to be "taught" how to play – they will not know what to do with blocks, sand, water, etc. They may never have had the chance to draw, paint and use scissors. However, once introduced to such experiences, they will quickly become engaged and enthralled by these opportunities – a mud slide being just one such possibility for these children at Daffodils Outdoor Nursery.

Your setting is the intervention

With increasing numbers of children entering settings with delayed development, particularly in speech, physical and social skills, it is becoming more common to see intervention groups occurring for younger and younger children. My message is that in the early years **your setting is the intervention**. A child should not be removed from one group and put into another in order that their needs can be met. In the best setting, the provision will meet the needs of all the children. Any extra funding (or extra adults) should be used within the main provision to *bring the intervention to the child*. Thus, a speech therapist should join a child in the sand to promote speech, a physiotherapist should use the outdoor area to support gross motor development and social skills are most powerful when taught "in the moment" in a real-life situation.

Specialist teachers

Similarly, specialist teachers should come into the setting, rather than taking children to a separate area for a specialist lesson. This is a very common occurrence in private schools, international schools, some private nurseries and during PPA cover in schools. It is preferable for the specialist teachers (whether they specialise in music, PE, ICT, RE, French, dance, etc.) to join the children in their child-initiated play and teach them as they are taught by the regular staff. The music teacher might then enhance the musical aspect of the play (introducing instruments to the story telling, for example); the Physical Education (PE) teacher can develop the ball skills of the group who have chosen to play football; the French teacher can simply talk French and the Religious Education (RE) teacher can work "in the moment" to develop aspects of RE that are age appropriate.

To summarise, behaviour will be calm and purposeful if:

- children have formed a trusting relationship with practitioners;
- induction is carefully planned and involves parents as much as possible;
- children have "settled" and feel secure and confident in the environment;
- the environment is superb (see Chapter 3);
- children have long periods of uninterrupted free-flow play;
- adults are free to interact with children as they play;
- there are a few rules, calmly and consistently enforced;
- group times are kept to a minimum and are truly engaging;
- staff take time to "teach" children how to play and socialise.

More and more young children are being diagnosed with "conditions", the symptoms of which are behaviour-related. This increase has corresponded directly with the formalisation and schoolification of the early years. Many settings try to get children to do things which are developmentally inappropriate, behaviour issues emerge and a diagnosis is sought. A far better approach is to change the practice, ensure it is appropriate for such young children and then see how the behaviour improves. Trust that children want to be engaged, let them play, join them in their play and prepare to be amazed!

ACTION PLAN

Review your transition and induction routines to see if they support the highest levels of well-being of the children.

Review your "timetable" and see if interruptions can be minimised.

Monitor levels of involvement and remove activities/sessions which deliver low-level involvement.

Remove focussed tasks – staff must be free to interact during child-initiated play sessions.

Ensure the "rules" are clear and simple and applied consistently and firmly by everyone.

Staple Hill Stars had a number of transitions during the sessions and these often interrupted the children's playing time. Following Anna's advice, we cut these down to a minimum and now only interrupt the session for lunch and home times. We have found the new approach promotes more engaged learning through play opportunities. With fewer transition times the sessions are less stressful for the staff and the trigger points for less desirable behaviour have been minimised, making the sessions much smoother and easier to manage.

All our play opportunities are now provided by children accessing their own learning using the resources, which have been carefully selected and displayed, in our engaging environment. The staff now skilfully scaffold learning by following the child's interests in their self-chosen activity rather than imposing the planned play/learning activity. This approach has also had a dramatic impact on behaviour. Two children previously subject to behaviour support plans no longer require them. They became engaged, focussed and in control of their own learning and have made huge leaps in development, especially in the areas of Personal, Social and Emotional Development.

Helen Clegg and **Leanne Ford**, joint owners and managers of Staple Hill Stars Pre-school, Bristol, **2017**

Sad it is for those children whose anxiety is so great that they cannot play. We may look upon the inability to join with other children in imagination and creative play as one of the surest signs of grave inner difficulties that will sooner or later seriously disturb the mental life. . .

He is in fact lost and bewildered if he has not the support of a firm framework of life ordered for him.

Susan Isaacs, *The Nursery Years*, Routledge & Kegan Paul, London, **1929**

3 | An enabling environment (including coverage of maths and literacy)

An outstanding early years setting is a complex organisation and the environment is one piece of the jigsaw. The environment can support all children to be fully engaged in purposeful play of their own choice and interest. There are some underlying principles and these are outlined below. However, it is the level of involvement of the children that should be your main measure of success. As you read this chapter, try to formulate a plan for the development of your environment and then, if necessary, try to fund-raise or find time to put the plan into action. If possible, involve the whole staff team in making the changes. A make-over day can be a superb team-building INSET day and, once involved in developing the environment, the staff take ownership and are more likely to help with maintenance going forward.

Individual interests

Practitioners realise that they have a legal requirement to meet the interests of each unique child and that this is also best practice. However, I worry that they are trying to do this by providing different resources for each emerging interest. This is just not possible and also unhelpful in terms of learning. For example, if you have children interested in pirates, caravans, outer space, the police, etc., you cannot possibly resource each interest. Think instead about how the resources that you choose to have in your setting can be used to meet all interests. For example, a cardboard box can be turned into a pirate ship, a caravan, a rocket or a police car. Blocks and Lego can be used in the same way. Therefore, look at the opportunities that your environment offers, the versatility of your resources and trust that the creativity of the children will lead them to find ways to explore their emerging interests.

Workshop set-up

I am advocating that child-initiated play should be happening for the vast majority of every session in early years and Year One. This means that children choose where to go and what to do from the moment they arrive – they initiate their own play and adults join them and support them in their pursuits. I visit many settings where practitioners say that the children can choose what to do, but the choice is limited by what the practitioners have already selected and put out. In order to support genuine choice, you need to have a **workshop** set-up. This means that in all areas, the resources are available and accessible to the children at all times, but nothing is set out. The children need to be able to select any resource and use it in the way that they wish (within the agreed boundaries as described in Chapter 2). Therefore, the **areas are clear, stocked and tidy at the start of the day**: the sand and water are free of equipment (but the resources are available next to these areas), the PE equipment is in its usual position at the edge of the area, etc. Remember – plastic will not rot in the rain so leave plastic resources out to save time. Shopping baskets, attached with cup hooks or cable ties, make fantastic storage units – the rain runs straight through and it washes the resources too! These can be used for storage of the following resources: sand, water, small PE equipment, gardening and digging tools, etc.

Similarly indoors, tables and carpet areas should be free of equipment, although the resources are available next to these areas. For example, the unit below contains a box of playdough and resources to be used with the playdough. It is placed near a table and the children can choose whether or not to go to this area and what to do if they do go there.

When an environment is organised in this way, the **children are in control of their learning**. They are able to select the area in which to play, the resources to use in that area and what to do with them. Obviously, their choices are limited by the areas and resources available and it is therefore crucial to have appropriate areas with varied, high quality, open-ended resources. It is also vital that the areas are well-stocked, tidy, clearly labelled or shadowed and arranged to allow optimum access. Each cohort of children will be different and their interests and curiosities will change over the period of the year. Staff should constantly review and reflect on the environment to see which areas are proving productive and which need altering. For example, if the large construction items are in a different area to the tools, the children are less likely to combine them, so perhaps consider moving them closer together. Often when staff make changes such as this, then the play immediately becomes more productive and the resources will be used together more often.

Shadowing of resources is used to aid tidying – as seen with the building tools above. The "shadows" are cut from coloured card or paper and glued to the shelf. Once the shelf is covered in stickyback plastic, the shadowing will remain in place for several years – a task worth doing! This shelving is an old bookcase and is another storage solution that is very useful. In the photograph, you can see that a tarpaulin has been attached which is pulled over the unit at night, secured in place with elasticated rope. Shelving like this can be used outdoors for musical instruments, investigation equipment, creative resources, and so on. Indoors, similar open shelving is the best option for most resources – a far better option than drawers or cupboards.

Because the children select and access resources themselves, they know where they are from and where to put them back when they have finished using them or at the end of the session. Thus, tidying up is far easier in settings organised in this way, compared to settings where the adults get the resources out for the children.

Outdoors all day

Thorley
Hill
Primary
School

Children should have access to the gardens from the moment they arrive. As mentioned before, 200 per cent more talking occurs outside and some children can only become deeply engaged in their play when they are outside. Staff need to value the outdoor space as much as, if not more than, the indoor space. Be very careful that you are not giving children subtle messages that outdoors is for "play" and indoors is for "work". Children read situations and will interpret them very well. If the teacher is always indoors, sat at a table, then the children will interpret this to mean that the teacher does not really value the experiences that the children are having outdoors. Boys, in particular, will achieve better results if they have more access to outdoors – so please open the doors and let the children outside, but make sure you go with them!

Plastic strips in the doorways keep the cold air out even when the doors are wide open – a worthwhile investment. If the door to your garden is closed at the start of the day, I would ask "why?" There is usually a way to solve any issues and I would urge settings to find ways to have the doors open immediately. Not only does the indoor space often get left untouched (and therefore tidy), but the levels of involvement will leap, meaning greater brain activity and greater progress over time.

Less is more

In many settings that I visit, there is far too much "stuff"! When working to develop an environment, the first task is usually to order a skip and get rid of all the rubbish, as well as resources that have not been used for years. We usually donate dozens of sacks of items to local charity shops, too, such as resources which have been duplicated (e.g. 20 sieves, 30 boats, etc.), dressing up costumes, plastic castles, pirate ships, construction toys that are too difficult or too easy for the children, and so on. When making these decisions, ask the following questions and, if the answer is yes, get rid of the item in question:

- Do children display low-level or no involvement with this resource? (For example, letters and numbers in the sand!)
- Do I have too many of these?
- Do I have other resources which serve the same purpose but which deliver better levels of involvement? (For example, many settings have many different construction toys and this is really not necessary.)
- Can this resource be made from other resources? For example, a farm, a hospital, a carpark, a zoo, can be made from the blocks or Lego. A batman costume can be made from fabric, or from paper and tape, in the creative area. However, animals, people, cars and trains are difficult to make, so these should be kept.
- Is this resource too difficult for the children to use? For example, Polydrons are very difficult for two year olds, but perfect for children in Year One.
- Is this resource too easy for the children to use? For example, tricycles in Reception!
- Can this resource only be used in one way? Try to ensure that most of the resources that you keep have scope for the children to be creative in their use. So, although jigsaw puzzles do have some value, you do not need too many of these. Similarly, outdoors, a fixed climbing frame has less value than equipment that can be moved and altered.
- Is this something that the children have easy access to at home? In particular, games and apps on screens are not necessary in settings – children have these at home. Try to ensure that you are giving the children experiences that they might not get at home.

"Less is more" is definitely a phrase to keep in mind: with fewer, carefully selected resources, they are well-used and easy to tidy up. If the resources are carefully selected, the majority can be used all year – the children will use them differently every day. In the photo above, showing the resources next to a water tray, the contents of the larger boxes on the bottom shelf can be changed to meet emerging interests.

Consistent and calm

It is a good idea to view your environment from the child's height – or, as seen in this photo, the baby's height.

Daffodils Outdoor Nursery

Once the environment is working (i.e. most of the children are deeply engaged for most of the day), then there is no need to keep changing it. Maintain the environment and restock consumables (wood, sand, etc.) but leave things the same. However, if the levels of involvement are low, then obviously things have to change. If you are seeing low levels of involvement, then the following questions might need to be asked and the issues addressed:

- Do the children have long periods of uninterrupted play? If not, can this be changed?
- Can the children be outdoors all day or, if not, for long periods of two hours or more?
- Are the resources open-ended (i.e. can they be used in infinite ways)? Examples include – fabric, blocks, sand, water, mud, natural resources, wood for woodwork, etc.
- Are the resources accessible to the children or do they have to ask for resources?
- Are there too many resources – meaning that the area becomes too chaotic and too difficult to tidy?
- Are the rules and boundaries simple and consistently enforced, ensuring that all the children feel relaxed in the setting?
- Is the area "zoned" to create numerous playing areas? Is the space too big/too small?
- Are there elements of risk in the environment which will challenge and engage the children – such as woodwork, rope swings, two-wheeler bikes, real tools?
- Can the children change the environment or is everything fixed? For example, is there a fixed climbing frame or are there A-frames, planks, tyres, etc. that the children can use?
- Are the adults as involved as the children? Are they interacting, scanning and maintaining the environment?
- Are there areas which will encourage wildlife and mini-beasts?

In the best settings, you will notice that it is calm. This is not to say that the children are passive – far from it. The children are deeply engaged and therefore the atmosphere feels calm and purposeful. Once this is achieved, then leave the environment alone. You do not need to add enhancements or change areas. Experience will soon show that if you do enhance an area, the children will all rush to that area and chaos will ensue. It is far better to wait and see if a new interest emerges and then work with the children to develop this interest at the time. For example, if a child talks about their cat at the vet, then this is the time for a "pop-up" vet surgery, set up with the children and with them becoming involved in making the resources that they need for this role play.

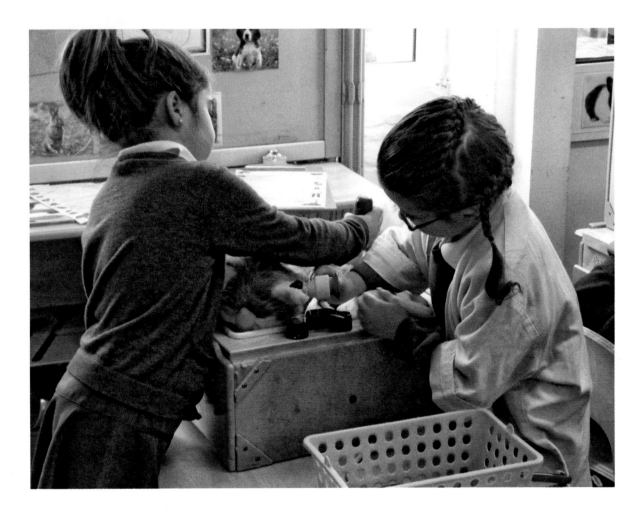

Displays too should be calm and simple. Many practitioners spend hours creating beautiful displays and I ask the question "Who do they benefit?" Hessian-backed boards with large photographs of children playing can be beautiful and, with appropriate captions, these can be enough to satisfy any visitors. Other boards, if they are at the children's height, can be used by them to display their creations if they wish and photographs of families are always interesting to them. Keep outside areas calm too – the children will bring the colour and energy.

Not too many labels

Another task which is a huge waste of time is that of labelling everything and adding "words" everywhere. For example, if you are asked to add words around the water tray, (as I was asked to do many times), then I would ask the question "Why do I need words around the water tray? Who are the words for, because the children cannot read them?" The response is often something like "Oh, they are not for the children. They are for the adults, so that they remember the vocabulary to introduce to the children." What an insult to the staff! We, as professionals, must challenge such requests and explain that a literate environment is not about having words and labels everywhere. Rather, it is about using literature in authentic ways so that children see the value and power of literacy. Therefore, have cookery books in the home corner, books about bridges in the construction area, books about guinea-pigs near the class pet, or (as seen in the photo below from The Nest Nurseries) books about the desert in a sand area.

Indoors and outdoors are different

An outdoor area should allow for learning in all areas of development, but should not mirror the indoors. The advantages of outdoors should be exploited – we can be much noisier, messier, bigger and faster outside. Therefore, this is the ideal place to have loud hammering and sawing, music and dancing, messy mud mixtures and challenging physical apparatus. It is also the place to learn about, and experience, the weather – wind, rain, snow or sun – and to explore the natural world of mini-beasts, pond life and plants – with a productive vegetable and fruit area being one of the most challenging but valuable possibilities. But possibly the most important learning that happens outdoors is the development of personal and social skills and self-regulation. In this large area, where the children have a great deal of independence and are able to take risks, they learn to negotiate, co-operate, assess possibilities and dangers and take control of their own learning. Also, communication and language develop at a greater pace than indoors and physical development, particularly gross motor development, is clearly easier to promote outdoors in large spaces and on large equipment, trees and logs and so on. The only area that I would duplicate outdoors is a reading area, somewhere cosy and protected from the wind, where children can look at fiction books. This is essential for those children who never choose to go indoors. All other aspects of learning can be covered outdoors with different equipment, but having opportunities to sit with an adult and look at a book should be available both indoors and outdoors.

The indoor area should also allow for learning in all areas of development, but should not mirror the outdoors. There are many advantages indoors that should be exploited. It

Reading opportunities outdoors   Non-fiction books outdoors

is dry, with a controllable temperature and no wind. Therefore, this is the ideal place for children to be calm and quiet (and staff should enforce this requirement firmly and consistently), pursuing activities which require small equipment and using resources that will not survive the outdoor elements.

Five minutes to set up

If a workshop set-up is developed, then indoors and outdoors should only take a few minutes to set up. Indoors, the water tray needs to be filled, the snack area prepared and the creative area restocked. The garden too should only take five minutes to set up and then it will be used every day. If it takes too long to set up you might decide not to use the space on some days. There are videos available on YouTube showing nursery, Reception and Year One gardens being set up in less than five minutes (search for "Anna Ephgrave" on YouTube.) The principle behind this is that as much as possible is left outside. If items are made of plastic, certain metals or natural substances (logs, pine cones, etc.) they can simply be left outside. If the resources are on shelves, the shelves can be covered with a tarpaulin. Anything very valuable (such as bicycles) might need to be locked away. A few items (such as books) might have to be brought out each day, but keep these to a minimum. Avoid having small items outdoors, such as little construction toys, etc., as these simply get lost. Equally, if the outdoor area is a very windy place then it can be very difficult to have paper outside, but make sure there is other mark-making equipment such as chalks, decorator's brushes to use with water, and so on.

Create zones

It is a good idea to try and break up large open spaces to create "zones" in an attempt to stop too much rampaging about (both indoors and outside). This proved particularly successful in the Reception garden shown below where a large expanse of flat concrete was zoned with sleepers containing woodchip, and planters placed around a small area of artificial grass. The transformation can be seen in the two photographs below.

Aim for authenticity whenever possible

Children respond to authentic resources and experiences. Therefore, keep this in mind when reflecting on your environment, the resources and the opportunities you offer. Real saucepans, for example, are easy to obtain and appeal to young children. By contrast, providing pumpkins, and golf tees for children to hammer into them, is not as engaging as wood and nails. When visiting a setting recently, a child came to the teacher with a handful of plastic numbers and said, "Someone put these in the sand – that was silly wasn't it? Don't worry I think I got them all out!" Shells would be found in sand – plastic numbers would not! The photo below shows the items under a sink in a role play area – authentic and therefore appealing. A real fire can cook food – a pretend one cannot.

These general principles apply to all ages. Environments need to be suitable for the age of the children, with resources that are well organised and that the children can **access independently** and many of which are **open-ended (versatile)**. An approach with a **"less is more"** attitude, and with **authenticity** in mind, will make practitioners be more selective about their resources. Babies need some different things to children in Year One and staff working with this age group will know what is appropriate in their rooms. However, I stress again, that it is the levels of involvement that should be your measure of success. If the children are showing high levels of involvement, then the environment is working – so leave it alone! If there is low-level involvement, then try to work out why this is the case.

Maths

The remainder of this chapter examines some specific areas indoors and outside. However, no maths area is mentioned. This is because I prefer to think of maths happening everywhere – just as personal and social development happens everywhere, so does communication and language, so does maths and so, indeed, do all areas of development.

Young children do not see maths (or any other subject) as distinct or separate from the everyday business of their play and exploration. It is just another aspect to their play and

occurs in every area of a setting. The grid below gives some examples and demonstrates how absurd it is to try and keep maths to a single area of a class or garden. I would also recommend having sets of Numicon shapes in all areas – in the playdough, the sand, the water, the mud kitchen, the role play area, the small construction area and displayed on the walls.

Area	Mathematical opportunities
Outdoor PE equipment area (chalk board attached to wall nearby)	Different size balls. Keeping count or score and comparing. Comparing/measuring distances jumped or distances travelled by a ball, etc. Ordinal numbers. Positional language.
Large and small-scale construction – including beads, cars, Lego, animals, etc.	Measurements of structures built. Shape, size and number of blocks (or other construction toy) used. Properties of various shapes. Positional language. Sorting and classifying cars, animals, etc. Creating patterns – symmetrical and repeating, sorting and ordering by size, colour, shape with beads, cars, etc.
Mud kitchen Water areas Sand areas Playdough Cooking	Capacity and associated language. Counting when creating/ following recipes. Comparing size and shape of containers and cutters. Creating patterns with stones, leaves, sticks, shells, candles, etc. Catching and counting fish, etc. Using balance and associated language. Matching shapes to shadows on shelves to tidy up.
Digging area	Counting legs on insects. Comparing length and thickness of worms. Language of size when digging holes.
Wheeled toys	Numicon and numeral attached for matching and numeral recognition in associated parking bays. Use of timer for turn-taking. Discussion and comparison of speed. Counting and comparison of wheels.
Music area	Bells ordered and numbered. Operating CD player – selecting numbered tracks. Counting beats on drum, etc. Creating patterns with sound.
Den building	Size, shape, height discussions. Counting pegs used/needed. Discussion about capacity of den built.

Area	Mathematical opportunities
Woodwork	Size, shape and related properties of various pieces of wood. Counting numbers of wheels, strings, windows, etc., needed for train, bike, guitar, etc. Understanding of weight of various pieces of wood and tools. Use of positional language.
Role play	Use of clocks, telephones, cookers, remote controls, money, balance, scales, recipe books, sets of plates and cutlery, etc., leading to discussion, experience and understanding of concepts associated with shape, space, measure and number.
Creative area	Shapes, size, number in creations – with boxes, collage, etc. Creating patterns. Sewing – size, shape of fabric and thread.
Self-register and visual timetable	Counting and comparing numbers of children. Developing language and concepts of time, and ordering of events.
Books, puzzles, games	Available in carpet areas and outdoor investigation and reading area and include topics such as shape, number, colour, time, size, etc.
Snack area	Shape, size of fruit. Capacity concepts with drinks. Fractions – one half, one quarter, etc.
Daily routines	Counting and numbers can be emphasised and developed during daily routines. For example, in Reception, when children are tidying up outside, they can be given a number card when it is time to line up and they then have to order themselves correctly in the line.

A word of warning – be very careful in the use of questions when interacting with young children. It is easy to spoil a meaningful experience with an inappropriate (often mathematical) question. For example, if a child is enacting a magical tale with a flying horse and a princess, then do not ask how many legs are on the horse! You may laugh, but that is exactly what I witnessed when visiting a nursery recently. The child looked up at the adult, put the horse back in the tray and went outside. Smart move!

Outdoor areas

In this section, some of the possible areas that you can have in an outdoor area are listed. They are listed in the order in which I value them (in terms of the levels of involvement that they deliver). Obviously, the age of the children in your setting will determine which sections are relevant and which are not. Readers, please trust your own judgement with regard to what is suitable for the children in your care.

It is a good idea to have a stock of **appropriate clothing and boots** for children (and adults!) to wear outdoors. Each setting needs to decide about the rules. For example, do the children have to wear boots in the mud, do they have to wear a coat in the rain? Whatever the rules, ensure that the adults are consistent and that the children are clear about the expectations. Have chairs available for children to sit on when changing their shoes and, if possible, provide fully waterproof clothing so that the weather will never prevent children from going outside. Remember the phrase: "No such thing as unsuitable weather – just unsuitable clothing."

Bits and pieces

This can mean many things but basically if you can acquire lots of items for the children to use outdoors, then, with adult support initially, the children will soon become creative and engaged in constructing infinite things such as dens, boats, motorbikes, aeroplanes, swimming pools – the possibilities are endless. Many useful items can be found but others

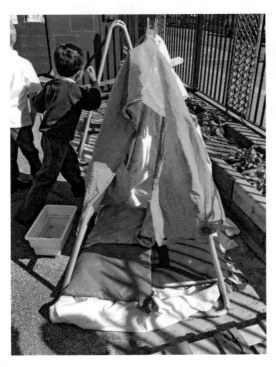

might need to be bought. Large blocks are very expensive but they deliver high levels of involvement and learning. They can be combined with numerous found and real resources, such as fabric, tyres, car parts, logs, ropes, crates, sticks, pegs, trays, pipes, carpet pieces, and so on. Start looking in skips and on building sites to see what treasures you can find. I have found several car bumpers at the side of the road, as well as hub caps and number plates. Old cable drums make great tables and bread trays combined with go-kart tyres make superb little vehicles. Children will use almost anything, and often in ways that adults would not anticipate.

Many of these resources can be left out in the open, at the edge of the area where they are to be used – logs, tyres, cable drums, pipes, etc. However, some things must be protected from the rain (and should not be used on rainy days). The large blocks are one such item – they are very expensive and easily ruined if they get wet. These can be stored in a simple shed and this can then be closed if it starts to rain. Other items, such as fabric, can be stored in salt bins – again easy to close if the weather changes.

Richmond Avenue, Nursery and Primary School, Southend

Space to run, jump and climb

Remember the rule is to walk indoors, and therefore a space to run outside is essential.

Gross motor skills can be developed with the use of large cable drums, logs, planks, crates and so on. Also, equipment such as A-frames, with ladders, a single pole, PE tables, steps and such like is useful. These can provide enough options and challenges for gross motor development to ensure that it is not necessary to go out of the garden for PE lessons. If a rope swing or a trapeze swing can be added to a tree as well, then even better. If there are two trees or posts, a rope bridge with two pieces of rope, one for the hands and one for the feet, can be made.

Bicycles have been mentioned, but remember to ensure that these do not dominate the whole outdoor area. Indeed, if the outdoor area is tiny, then consider not having bikes. If you do have bikes, then ensure a variety – gliders, two-wheelers and trikes – and keep them to a clearly defined area. If you do have a large amount of money to invest, then avoid fixed climbing equipment as children quickly bore of the same thing every day. The only fixed equipment that I would advocate are monkey bars, ropes and rope swings as mentioned above, or a trapeze as shown below.

Smaller equipment (bats, balls, skipping ropes, stilts, hoops, beanbags, etc.) can be stored in baskets outside and these can support the development of finer motor control.

Woodwork

If we could scan the brain of this child, we would see great activity – powerful learning and rapid progress. Such deep-level involvement is always found at the woodwork benches.

"Risk Assessments", by their nature, focus on the negative aspects of an activity. I always prefer to write a "Benefit/Risk Assessment". In this way, the focus is on why you are doing a particular activity before thinking about the possible risks and how to mitigate them. The assessment below demonstrates clearly that the benefits of woodwork far outweigh the risks.

Benefits

Woodwork is the perfect activity in which children can demonstrate the characteristics of effective learning:

playing and exploring – children investigate and experience things, and "have a go";
active learning – children concentrate and keep on trying if they encounter difficulties, and enjoy achievements; and
creating and thinking critically – children have and develop their own ideas, make links between ideas, and develop strategies for doing things.

Also, all the seven areas of learning in the current EYFS framework will be developed:

Physical development: with the use of real tools and hard wood (rather than balsa wood), the muscles in the hands and arms become stronger and the children develop more control of these muscles. They learn to vary the amount of force used – with hammers and saws. They also develop hand-eye co-ordination in order to hit the nails. Fine motor control is developed as children hold the thin nails in place. Through experience they learn how to keep their fingers out of the way of the hammer.

Personal, social and emotional development: children demonstrate deep levels of involvement when undertaking a woodwork task. Often, children who normally will not persevere at a task are prepared to try for far longer at woodwork – perhaps because they realise it is something truly challenging but also "real". Children will return to unfinished work the following day if necessary. They learn to share and take turns, negotiating and discussing routines and rules. They learn how to keep themselves and others safe. They realise that a real hammer can do serious harm and they treat the tools with respect. They learn to follow agreed rules. Children who find it difficult to conform are often so keen to participate that they do manage to comply with requests and boundaries at the woodwork bench – just so that they get their turn. They take great pride in their achievements and therefore their self-esteem is boosted. For most children woodwork is a new activity and therefore they are taking a risk just by becoming involved – they take further risks using the equipment but learn to do this safely and independently and the results are greatly appreciated.

Caldecote Primary School, Leicester

Communication and language development: there is always a lot of discussion at the work bench and therefore language is developed. Children have to follow instructions and will often be heard explaining the rules to other children. They encounter problems all the time and discuss solutions. They explain what they are doing and learn the vocabulary associated with the activity.

Creative development: with many activities for young children, the process is as important (if not more important) than the product. This is definitely the case when children are first starting at woodwork. They need to develop the techniques. Eventually, they will start to use their imagination, combined with their knowledge of the task, to plan what to make. With support, they will have learnt how it is possible to combine various materials and media and this will increase their options and possibilities. Many of the models become the starting point for a story which also supports creative development (as well as language skills).

Knowledge of the world: clearly through working with wood, the children will learn about its properties and the properties of other materials that they combine with the wood. They will learn about how to use tools and how to combine different materials. With appropriate interactions, they could learn about the source of wood and various types of wood. They will be experiencing the process of "design, make, review".

Mathematical development: this pervades every aspect of the task – from experiencing the weight and size of the wood to deciding how many wheels to add to a truck. Children will be thinking about size and shape, as well as number. Again, with appropriate interaction, their thoughts can be vocalised, refined and developed.

Literacy development: children will often combine mark-making with woodwork – adding drawn features to their models. They also add their name to ensure their work is not lost. They will use books to refer to for ideas or information. Also, as mentioned above, many models will feature in stories and the literacy possibilities within this are infinite (story scribing is explained later in this chapter).

There are not many activities which appeal to so many children and have such broad and deep learning potential.

Risks and actions

Hazard	Possible scale of injury	Precautions to put in place to reduce risk	Risk rating
General risk of injury through use and misuse of tools	Medium	Staff will ensure close supervision of children during the induction period until all children have been trained in the use of the tools and comply with the "2 children at each bench" rule. Staff will then remain vigilant in watching the woodwork area. Adults all aware of how to get first aid help if necessary.	Low
Children with behavioural difficulties/ developmental delay might not adhere to the rules and might not use the tools safely	Medium	Staff will ensure close supervision of these children if they are near the woodwork area.	Low
Sawdust in eyes	Low	Children to wear goggles on windy days.	Low
Hit fingers with hammer	Low	Train children to tap lightly to fix nail in place and then move hand away when they hit harder.	Low
Children get hit by moving tools	Medium	Strict imposition of two-children-only limit at the bench. Staff will scan and monitor the area at all times.	Low
Cut with saw	Low	Strict rule – "wood in vice".	Low
Splinters	Low	Wood will be checked. Children shown how to use sandpaper.	Low
Sharp nails cause injury	Low	Protruding nails will be hammered down. Children will not remove nails from work area.	Low

Clearly the benefits are great and the risks can be managed.

(It should be noted that where woodwork has been introduced there have never been any serious accidents at the woodwork benches and rarely even minor incidents.)

Practicalities

Induction and access: the benches should be outdoors (the noise would be unbearable indoors) and in an area that can be seen at all times. When the children first start, woodwork should be available immediately and with an adult beside the bench at all times. Staff should encourage parents to help ensure that the children adhere to the very simple rules: two children at each bench, two hands on the saw. There must be zero tolerance of any dangerous behaviour and the children quickly learn to behave appropriately if they want to be involved. The woodwork should be part of the continuous, outstanding provision – always available and, therefore, not causing a "mad rush" of children trying to have a turn. After the induction period, adults should "keep an eye" on the woodwork area, but an adult does not always need to be "stationed" there.

Equipment: I would recommend small claw hammers, smooth fine nails (bought by the kilo from an ironmonger) and adult-size hack-saws. The work bench from *Creative Cascade UK Ltd.* is sturdy and very reasonably priced.

Additional resources: a variety of resources can be added for children to fix to the wood such as milk bottle tops, elastic bands, fabric, corex, corks, buttons, string, etc. Paint, felt pens and pencils should be available to decorate models as well.

Wood: wood is too expensive to buy. The best option is to find a local timber merchant who offers a cutting service for customers. They are usually happy to keep off-cuts for use in school or nursery – a large bin can be taken to the timber yard which is filled up with off-cuts and the wood can then be collected every few weeks.

Woodwork leads to deep learning and outstanding progress in all areas of development. Children are attracted to the challenges it brings and fascinated by the possibilities. Adults can be anxious about this activity but I would urge settings to have a go – the resulting engagement and learning will amaze and delight adults and children alike.

Investigation of the natural world

In many settings that I visit I find an unopened box of magnifying glasses in the cupboard. They are not doing much good in a cupboard. Bring them outside and let the children use them. It is easy to set up some outdoor shelving with bug boxes, magnifying glasses, spades and so on so that the children can explore and study the mini-beasts that they find. Try to find a space that will encourage such creatures into your garden. The smallest area of earth, with some logs or pieces of carpet will deliver some exciting discoveries. If you can introduce other animals to your setting, this is one of the richest learning experiences for young children. Chickens (possibly even hatched from eggs), guinea-pigs, rabbits and fish are all quite easy to keep and advice is available from many organisations. Add a box of information books nearby so that these can be referred to if the children find a creature or ask a question.

Obviously, the weather is a free resource outdoors, so celebrate this and use it. The children will be excited by the wind and will be engaged, running around with ribbons or making kites. Puddles from the rain deliver endless possibilities, and shelters to get out of the rain are always challenging and fun to build. Snow is magical and in the heat of the sun, a paddling pool made from tarpaulin will keep a large group busy for hours.

If you have space for even the smallest **growing area**, then this too has huge potential for engagement and learning. By involving the children at every stage of the process, the work can be shared and the results are then even more exciting.

September

July

Sand

This area is one of the most popular outdoors, but the sandpit needs to be big enough for the children to get **into** the sand if possible. A huge sandpit can easily be built from treated sleepers. The sleepers are relatively cheap to buy and can be placed directly onto a hard surface. Fixings are not essential as the sleepers are so heavy that small children cannot usually move them. Washed silver sand is ideal to fill the area and resources need to be stored nearby. Metal shopping baskets can be attached to a fence – just hooked onto cup hooks – with a photo and word above each basket to help with tidying up. These baskets are fantastic as they can be left outside all the time – the resources are plastic or natural and the rain goes through the baskets. If you have a mesh fence, the baskets can be attached with cable ties, or even just placed on the ground around the sand pit. The baskets can contain buckets, spades, vehicles, moulds, sieves, natural resources (shells, conkers, twigs, stones, bark, etc.). It is a good idea to have another unit nearby with plates, cutlery, saucepans etc. for the inevitable cooking that takes place, along with a small table and chairs to promote role play. If possible, attach pulleys to a fence, or to any shelter above the sand, and also have a large hanging balance. The sand pit can be covered with a tarpaulin at night, held in place with tyres placed on top. Another, preferable, option is netting, which deters cats and other visitors, but which lets the rain through.

The sand outdoors will usually be wet, either from rain or from water transported to the area by the children. This allows for sand castles, cakes, stews, volcanoes, tunnels, rivers, mountains, and so on, to be built.

You will observe high levels of involvement in this area – children are fascinated by sand, its properties and its potential. I often advise practitioners to spend a day in the sand pit to observe the children carefully in their play and find out why they are so fascinated. Do not worry about children who stay in one area for long periods or who repeatedly return to an area. Remember, they would not stay there if they were bored. But in order to understand what is engaging them, you need to take the time to observe their play.

Water

Shopping baskets again are ideal for storage of water resources. As explained above, there is no need to set up the water area – the resources are left in place, ready to be used. Resources could include buckets, jugs, funnels, pipes, brushes, sponges, bottles, boats, water animals, etc. A Creative Cascade Set, with stands and guttering, can be used to create water channels. Children will inevitably transport the water to water plants, wet the sand, mix with mud, pour down the pipes, fill saucepans and many other things. A water butt is a great way to give the children access to water independently – even if it has to be filled every day with a hose.

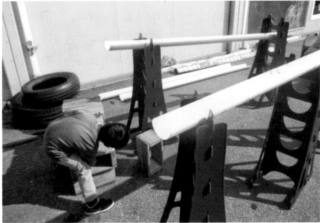

Mud and mixtures

If you have space, then you can have sand, water *and* mud for the children to explore. The two photographs above show the same corner before and after development at St Mary's Primary School in Whitstable. Improvements were made with a plain wall, simpler storage, removal of unnecessary tarpaulin and the creation of a simple table. Domestic role play will emerge in all these areas, so it is a good idea to have the pots, pans, plates and utensils to support this. Also, have some good gardening tools so that the children can successfully dig and, again, ensure there is a water supply nearby. I would advise containing the mud in something, rather than just using mud in the ground, otherwise there is a tendency for the mud area to expand and the whole garden to become a quagmire.

In the two photographs below, one in the garden of a childminder, there is no mud but there are stones, sticks, pine cones, grass, bark, leaves and so on which are all equally engaging, with infinite possibilities.

Music and dancing

Another area that is far better suited to outdoors is music and dancing. A simple stage can be constructed from two pallets, with decking strips screwed down to cover the top. Simpler still is some ready-made decking pieces. Once placed near a wall, with a shower curtain as a backdrop, the stage is set. Instruments on shelving nearby as well as fabric to make costumes encourages wonderful shows. Song books nearby can be useful and, for older children, it is possible to write out simple tunes for them to play on bells and other tuned instruments.

Creative/mark-making/writing

It is possible to have creative and mark-making resources outside and this is a lot easier if your garden is protected from the wind and if you have a shelter. However, if your garden is a wind tunnel without a shelter, then you might decide that it is too difficult to store paper outdoors. If this is the case, then try to ensure that there are alternative creative opportunities outdoors – such as decorator's brushes to use with water, chalks to use on the floor or a blackboard, etc. Also, paper can be put on clip boards and mark-making equipment in tool belts or rucksacks for the children to carry around.

Reading area

As mentioned above, the only area that I would replicate outdoors would be a book area – somewhere cosy and comfortable that children can look at fiction books, either with an adult or with their friends.

Role play

Children will engage in role play everywhere but, if a new interest emerges, then it can be beneficial to set up a particular role play area outdoors. This can often compliment the "home corner" that, I believe, should be constantly available (and might be indoors, outside or both). Therefore, if a child starts talking about the café, the vet, the car wash or the police station, then this can be developed outside, using the open-ended resources described above. Signs and other special resources can then be made or gathered up, involving the children at every stage. Once interest in the area declines, then it is easily dismantled or changed. Doll's buggies are one resource which it is easier to have outdoors, where there is often more space than indoors. Again, a staff team must agree on the rules and then stick to them. I have always had the rule that indoor resources stay indoors and outdoor resources stay outdoors. This is not what would happen in Utopia but, with limited budgets, it is the best option.

Extras

Throughout my career, I have found or been offered items that I have used in my settings. For example, my neighbour gave me a fibreglass boat and a friend gave me a caravan. If your outdoor area is large, then it would be crazy to refuse such things. When working with the Oasis Academy Hobmoor in Birmingham, staff chose to buy a caravan and a boat (shown below) to support the opportunities for role play in the lovely large outdoor area.

Outdoor area for 60 Reception children at St Mary's Primary
School, Whitstable, Kent

With tiny outdoor areas – ask "What can I *not* have indoors?" and use the answer to
guide you.

Tiny outdoor areas

If your outdoor area is very small, then try to include the following (always bearing
in mind that whatever is on offer indoors will be used in combination with your
outdoor area):

- Bits and pieces (blocks, fabric, crates, tyres, pipes, rope, planks, boxes, etc.)
- Woodwork area
- Musical instruments
- Sand
- Water
- Equipment to develop gross motor skills (A-frames, bats and balls, skipping ropes, etc.)
- Equipment to investigate the natural world

Indoor areas

When considering "authenticity", try to think what it would mean to the children in your setting. "Authentic" does not mean items from the 1920s. However, china cups are more authentic than plastic ones. Aim for a "homely" feeling, but not a museum. In the photo here, we see a real wooden table, crockery and utensils, all of which the children can handle and use – and all sourced from boot sales and charity shops by the staff at The Nest Nurseries. Staff need to feel confident that the benefit of such resources outweighs any potential risks. For example, very thin glass items would not be appropriate. Equally, although a plastic bucket in the sand is not 'beautiful', it is totally functional and appropriate.

As with outdoors, staff should review and reflect on the environment to see which areas are proving productive and which need altering. Remember the principles – accessible, versatile resources; less is more; aim for authenticity. The **layout** of the indoors can be challenging and staff need to reflect on which areas are causing a lot of stress, why this is the case and what can be done to reduce this. There is often too much furniture indoors, in particular **too many tables** and chairs and the simple solution to this is to get rid of the ones that are not essential. If rooms are used for meal times, then try to source tables with removable or collapsible legs so that they do not have to be in the room all day. Carpet flooring is also a big cause of stress. **Wood, laminate or lino** are preferable because they allow the room to be arranged in any way, rather than being restricted by the location of the flooring areas that can be mopped easily. Think carefully about the location of different resources. For example, although it is essential to have opportunities for mixing sand and water outside, you might want the indoor sand to be dry in order to offer different opportunities. Therefore, it is necessary to keep the water tray and equipment away from the sand tray. Staff might want to avoid making new playdough every day – so this also needs to be placed away from the water and sand. Once you identify stressful areas in the room, start asking questions. Is the construction area too small and over-crowded? If so, can it be moved or expanded? Are the children tripping over the chairs? If so, are the chairs necessary? Children are often happy standing at tables or kneeling on the floor. Do children keep knocking down other children's models as they walk past? If so, can the construction area be protected with units in some way? Do children keep leaving rubbish on the creative table? If so, is there a bin nearby? These seem like obvious questions and obvious solutions, but it is amazing how practitioners just learn to live with such aggravations, without trying to find solutions.

As with outdoors, I look at some possible indoor areas that can be developed. Again, please think carefully about the stage of development of your children. You know them best and you know what will be appropriate, challenging and interesting to them.

Playdough

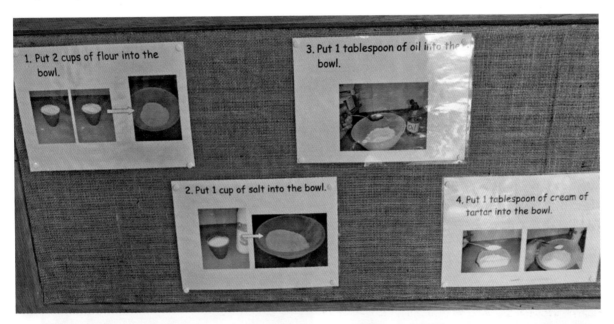

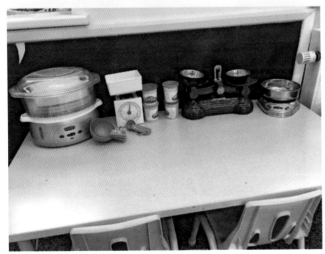

Playdough-making station, Richmond Avenue Primary School

It never ceases to amaze me how children will play with playdough every day. On p. 37 of this chapter there is a photograph of a shelving unit containing playdough and associated resources. It is worth spending time to create such a unit as it will be in permanent use. Look carefully at the photo to see the variety of resources, but also note the "less is more" approach. Two pairs of scissors, rather than 20. A few cutters rather than many, etc. There is a recipe for playdough available in Appendix B.

Many settings have developed a playdough station (as shown in the photograph above) where children can make their own playdough whenever necessary.

Cooking

The play at the playdough table, in the mud, in the sand and in the home corner is often concerned with cooking, something which children see happening at home. The obvious development of this play is to do some real cooking and this is an activity which delivers deep levels of involvement and, therefore, learning. If possible, create an area where cooking can happen within your room. Even if the actual cooker is elsewhere, the preparation can be done in the room. Many simple recipes can be developed that children as young as three can follow independently. Two such recipes are available in Appendices C and D. As children get older (especially in Year One), they can design their own dishes, write ingredient lists and instructions, buy the ingredients, make the dish and then review the finished product as shown in the example below. Anyone who knows the content of the Year One curriculum will realise that vast amounts can be covered by this sort of activity.

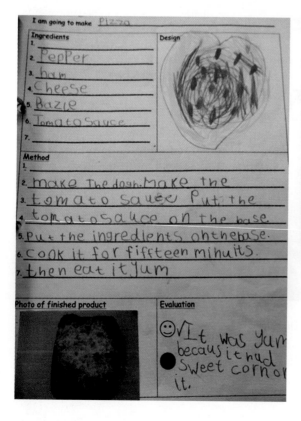

Creative/mark-making

Creative development covers numerous activities from role play to painting to singing to making up stories, but I am concentrating here on the "art" aspect of creativity: mark-making, sewing, model making, etc.

 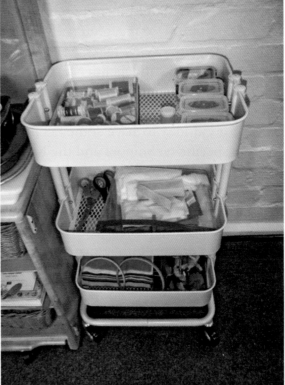

Brindishe Green Primary School, Lewisham

As with maths, I would not usually suggest having a "writing area" that is separate from other mark-making because young children do not separate their learning and play into distinct subjects. They will make a beautiful card and then write a message inside; they will "write" a shopping list and draw some of the items; they will make a robot, paint it and then "write" a story about it. Mark-making will combine elements of drawing and writing and therefore all the resources for it can be stored in one large area, with one large table. This can be replicated outside if the outdoor area is suitable, although with fewer collage materials, etc., as they blow away!

Re-stocking the creative areas is a time-consuming task. As with all areas, the equipment should be shadowed or labelled with a photo and word to ensure that the children can tidy up independently. Tilted storage boxes are useful for collage materials and the Ikea kitchen rails and pots are great for pencils and pens, etc., and also for sewing equipment. Junk modelling boxes can be displayed on shelves along with an assortment of paper and card. Other resources should include scissors, sticky tape in dispensers, staplers, hole punches, sewing equipment, string, glue (various types), fabric and wool. Easels are useful indoors and outside, with drying racks. Many settings use ready-mixed paint (storing this in soap dispensers supports independence), but many have developed a system which allows the children to successfully mix their own powder paints. For example, I saw nursery children dispensing powder paint stored in sugar shakers in Larkhill Nursery School in Stockport.

It is a good idea to have some "craft" books in the creative area so that children can research specific techniques and the books also give them ideas if they wish. It is amazing how ambitious young children can be. Sewing, in particular, is very appealing to young children, and when children have had this experience in nursery, Reception and Year One, they become very skilled. The adults are used by the children for the parts of the process that they cannot do independently – often this includes threading the needle and tying a knot – but gradually they master the whole process. This pencil case was made in Year One, totally independently!

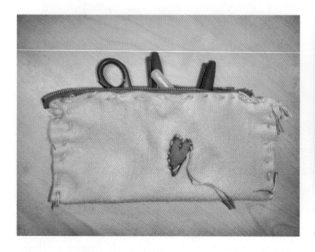

Literacy

As mentioned above, young children do not segment their learning by subject. This applies to literacy as much as to any other subject. In Chapter 1, brain development was discussed in a very simplistic way – as my colleague, Ruth Moore, says, "we are not neuroscientists." However, I do not need brain scans or scientists to confirm what experience with thousands of children has shown me – that children can learn to read and write in 12 weeks when they are at an appropriate stage of development. I have seen this happen in Year Two on several occasions in my career. Children who join an English school in Year 2 (age six or seven), and who have not had formal schooling in their own country, will learn to read and write in 12 weeks, often surpassing their peers who have become disengaged by seven years of the English education system. Chapter 1 also stressed how important the prime areas are. The prime areas underpin everything that is needed for a child to become literate – confidence (PSE), speech (CLL) and dexterity (PhD). There is a detailed section about speech and language development in Chapter 4, stressing that much of the teaching in the early years focuses on this area of development. However, I know that Reception teachers reading this book will be panicking and thinking "but what about the reading and writing"? I am therefore including some information about reading and writing here, so that readers can feel confident that these areas of learning can be addressed without compromising the child-led pedagogy.

We must remember that reading and writing are not an end in themselves, they are a means to an end. This vital point is being ignored in many schools where children are being forced to read and write at younger and younger ages, purely for the sake of passing a test. It is not surprising that they do not like writing very much and that they do not opt to write when they are able to choose what to do. However, in the very best settings, children choose to write for various reasons: to remember what to buy at the shop, to remember what to put in the cake, to create a wonderful story that will be read to the class and acted out, to send a message to their mum or a friend, to ask the site staff to do a job, to ask the head teacher for a new resource, to give instructions about something, to keep the scores in a game, to make sure everyone knows who a masterpiece belongs to, to know which fruit and vegetables are growing, etc. Thus, they write shopping lists, recipes, stories, letters, notices, score sheets, labels, etc. No wonder, then, that there are always children writing in such settings. These children are NEVER told to write, but they have seen the purpose and outcomes that writing can deliver and, therefore, they WANT to write. Of course, each time they write, they are **reading** what they have written. Thus, reading and writing develop together. On every occasion that a child shows an interest in writing something – be that a shopping list, a letter, a recipe, some instructions, a sign, etc. – the adult should **offer to write *for* the child.** As soon as you offer to do the physical part of the process, you will see children engage in the process because they can succeed. They can give you the words and maybe even some of the sounds. They can tell you how to form some of the letters but all the anxiety is removed from the process, making it enjoyable! So – **take the pencil from the child and write for them!** Watch their faces light up and watch how writing will "take off" in your setting. Gradually, as the children develop, they will relish the chance to write for themselves, rather than being afraid of the task.

As explained, the resources to support "writing" should be in all areas, including clip boards so that the children can take paper and pens to any areas they wish. I would not opt to have a "writing area" because young children do not see writing as something separate from their normal activity – it is just another part of their play. However, the resources should always be to hand, clearly labelled, well-stocked and with a wide variety of mark-making implements, paper, note books and card.

Story scribing and acting

Writing, writing, writing – every setting is worried about progress in writing. However, children can make outstanding progress in their writing – and the key is **never tell them to write!** I repeat **– never tell the children to write**. Wait for a moment when a child is interested in writing and then "pounce"! When a child is motivated to do something, that is the moment when support and teaching will be most powerful.

One exciting thing to introduce is story scribing, which I first heard about from Vivien Gussin Paley. Whenever the staff feel it is appropriate, you can offer to scribe a story for a child. Quite often it is just a drawing that will be the initial stimulus for a story – a butterfly, a princess, a monster or a rocket. Something a child has made can be brought into a story, small world play will have a storyline, as will the role play in the outdoor areas. When writing the story, it is important for the child to watch the adult write and for the adult to write exactly what the child says. In this way, even the youngest child learns that their spoken words can be transferred onto paper. They also see how writing is formed and what it looks like. The exact words that the child says are written down, even if grammatically incorrect (as evidence of the child's language at this time).

The following prompt sheet will help staff to support the children appropriately:

Story scribing

- Sit beside the child (if you are right handed, put the child on your left).
- Make sure the child watches you write (i.e. the paper should be in front of the child if possible). Write exactly what the child says.
- Use your knowledge of each child to decide which teaching is appropriate.
- Say the words as you write them.
- Sometimes stop and read what you have written and then let the child carry on.
- Sound out some words as you write them.
- Point out spaces, capitals and full stops, etc.
- Exaggerate some letter formation.
- Ask the child to sound out some words for you.
- Ask the child to write a few letters – or words – as appropriate to the individual child.
- Use terms such as "characters", "author", etc.
- The story is the important part – keep the momentum – the teaching should not slow down the scribing too much.
- DON'T FORGET TO ACT OUT THE STORY!!

For some children, it will be appropriate to suggest that they add their name at the end of the story. As the year progresses, there might be a few children in the nursery year who are able and keen to write a few other letters or words within their story. In Reception, the adults can offer the child the pen so that they can write a few of the sounds, words and eventually phrases that they are capable of. Thus, it becomes a shared writing process. In mixed-age classes, the older children can scribe for the younger children.

At the end of the session (morning or afternoon), the stories are shown to the group and an adult selects some children to act as the characters in the story. The story is then

read aloud and the children "act" the story. When this activity is first introduced, and the children see a story being acted out, then many more of them will be keen to write a story the next day.

The stories are kept in the children's folders or special books and become a record of their language development, their story-writing development, their imagination, sometimes their understanding of the world (depending on the content of the story), their pencil control (if there is a picture or if they have added their name) and, in Reception, a record of their phonics and writing development. For example, the following stories (and many others) appear in one **nursery child's folder** (all the writing in these stories was done by an adult):

November: "I am butterfly. I fly. I go home." The end.

January: "I am a butterfly and I always fly. I fly to little Africa and you have to play there. And then we finished. We go back to our home." The end.

March: "One day there was a little, little butterfly. He fly to little toy's house. Then he hop in the car and drive away to Africa. When he is finished in Africa he fly back home. Then there were two little fairies. They find a flying pony and fly all the way to the moon. Then when it's finished they fly back home." The end.

May: "One night a flying boat with magic sleeped and woke up, had lunch. He went in the forest. Then he fly into the down, down, down, down and goes deeped where the forest is. He found the very mean dragon and killed it, he was evil. He used the magical thing to kill it. And he fly back home and had the milk." The end.

July: "There was a big, big tiger. He was friendly and there was a friendly bat and a friendly bear. They found some friends to play with. They flied through the forest and to the moon. They lived there. Then they found a rainbow and flied to the end of it and found a treasure and went back home." The end.

In Reception classes the progress is dramatic too. The next series of photographs shows a few of the stories from one boy's folder. His first stories were also completely written by an adult (and I have not included them). In the first story shown here a few sounds have been written by the child. In the next story, a few words have been written and, in the next story, a few phrases. By the end of the year Joey was writing the complete stories himself. This evidence is replicated in many settings that have introduced this approach to writing and it is one of the main things that has impressed Ofsted inspectors around the country.

Reception children should have ten or 15 minute phonics sessions each day – short, intense teaching sessions – giving them the phonics knowledge that they can then apply as they choose. For children in settings before Reception – nursery, pre-school, day care – staff should introduce Phase One phonics within every aspect of the day. Each time they speak, read a story, sing a song, listen to the birds, they are delivering aspects of Phase One phonics. This does not need to be done through "phonics sessions". It should be done throughout the day within the play. This will eventually lead to oral skills of blending and segmenting, but this does not mean relating sounds to particular letters – leave that to Reception. **In Reception, cued articulation combined with a systematic introduction to the sounds has proved very successful.** Forty-five minute phonics sessions do not fit with the requirements of our statutory curriculum and staff should refuse to deliver such sessions. They are developmentally inappropriate and children who are subject to such sessions are demonstrating a real dislike for literacy. In contrast, children who have had skilled teaching and exciting, **authentic**, opportunities to write within their play, have a love of literacy. With this in mind, remember that if you are going to try story scribing, the acting-out of the stories is the most important thing for the children. It is this part of the process that will engage and inspire other children to want to write.

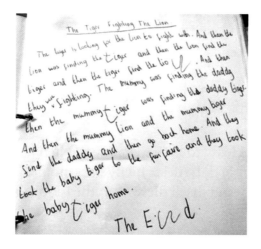

November

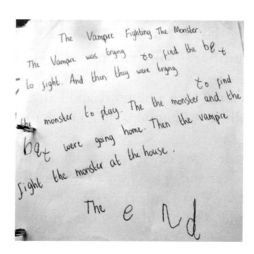

December

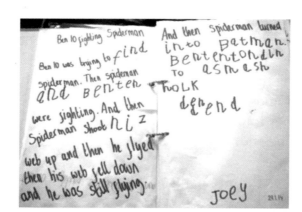

January

March

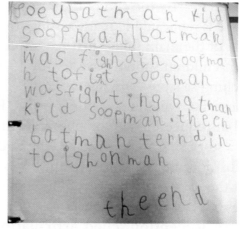

June

With the "top-down" pressure in schools, it is easy to become anxious and to try and "force" the writing but experience has shown that the wait is worthwhile. Story scribing – and indeed scribing for a child at any moment that they need something written – is a fantastic way to motivate children to want to write. It is also a great way to teach them about the process of writing well before they may be physically able to do any writing themselves. Starting formal teaching of writing at an earlier age **does not** lead to higher academic attainment at a later age. Indeed, putting pressure on young children to read and write before they are developmentally ready and before they are interested can have the opposite effect – it can put them off literacy activities for life. We must aim to do the reverse – to make children so fascinated and excited about what can be achieved by reading and writing that they are nagging us to have a go – **never us nagging them!!** Take the pressure off the children, offer to **write for them** and make sure the writing has a purpose.

Reading

Reading is another hugely contentious issue for Reception teachers in England. Again, the main message is to take the pressure off the children, read for them, let them see the power of reading and give them the knowledge and skills appropriate to their stage of development. Writing and reading are inextricably linked – each time we write, we read what we are writing. It is therefore important to model this when scribing for the children. Model how to read back what has been written. I would prefer the more "formal" teaching of reading to be left until the children are six, but in England, at this time, I realise that the pressures are huge. If you do have to introduce direct teaching of reading in Reception, then the following is a brief description of a model that is extremely effective and manageable.

When Phase Two phonics is started in Reception (usually around October half-term), it quickly becomes apparent that some children are developmentally ready and able to blend and segment – reading and making cvc words such as "sat" or "tip", etc. I would select six of these children to start the reading scheme and give them some one-to-one attention once per week to support this. This individual session does need to be with a skilled and sensitive member of staff at this critical stage. One adult can complete such sessions in about an hour and therefore, it is only one hour in the week which is disrupted by this activity taking place. After about six weeks, this group of six children can be handed to a volunteer who can carry out these individual sessions, and the next group can be selected and given individual reading books, supported by a member of staff. As the year progresses, more and more children will be developing and moving onto this system. However, never forget that some children are developmentally very young and it will not be appropriate for them to be doing this. They can be put off reading for life if they are pushed to read when it is not appropriate. Ensure that they retain a love of reading by showing them the power of text – i.e. **read to the children.**

Snack area

Since we want children to be as independent as possible and to have long periods of time to become absorbed in their pursuits, we should not dictate when they have a drink or snack. Therefore, I would recommend having a "snack area" where a few children can go at any time to have a drink (of water or milk) and a snack of fruit or salad items (carrots or tomatoes). This could be offered outdoors as well.

Many settings still have whole group/class snack time and I have seen extremely low levels of involvement during such sessions as children wait for the bowl of fruit to reach them. Many practitioners worry that some children will not eat and that others will take too much. Surely this then is a teaching and learning opportunity. Once established, a snack area can be totally self-regulating with children taking drinks and snacks that they need, without over-eating. If children are staying in a setting all day, then you might consider removing the snack area at a set time before lunch.

Small world/construction/carpet area

If your setting caters to large numbers of children in one space, then it is usually advisable to create two or more carpet areas so that children can be split for group times and also in order to create separate areas at other times.

However, do make sure to avoid "dead spaces", meaning spaces that are only used for group times, as this will mean that they are empty for the vast majority of the session. Wherever the carpet areas are, make sure they are used all the time. Clear floor space (carpeted or not) can be used for numerous activities and the necessary resources need to be stored around the edge of the carpet. As the photograph below shows, the storage units serve the extra purpose of creating a protective barrier around the carpet. This helps to prevent children walking across the carpet (and possibly spoiling a wonderful creation) and it helps to keep the resources contained within the area. In addition, at home time, it helps to contain the children until their parents arrive. In this example, there are just two "exit" points from the carpet so that it is easy for staff to monitor who is leaving the carpet area to go a parent.

The resources stored around the carpet could be as listed below. It is not necessary to have many different construction toys and it is not necessary to keep changing what is on offer. The white unit near the window is from Ikea – very reasonably priced and very sturdy. Other storage units appear in photographs throughout the book. Resources will, of course, vary with the age of the children.

- Construction toys (Duplo, small Lego, community blocks (small and mini sets)
- Wooden train set
- Cars and other vehicles
- People
- Numicon
- Books – reference and fiction
- Animals – dinosaurs, wild animals, farm animals, sea animals, etc.
- Natural resources – stones, pine cones, sticks, shells, etc.
- Variety of fabric pieces
- Electronic toys
- A few puzzles, games, threading toys, stacking toys, etc (as appropriate to the age of children)

Clearly this list invites an infinite variety of activities. However, review the area and add or remove resources if levels of involvement drop. Staff should also insist that children tidy away the resources that they have been using before they leave the carpet. In this way it remains inviting for others.

If you are able to have a second carpet area, this could be where the main book area is (including story props and puppets), a sofa, the "pop-up" role play area, and storage units for some individual folders.

Book area

A lovely book area is essential and should be made as inviting as possible. If there is enough space, have a sofa, cushions, puppets and props to make the experience engaging. You can also have books in numerous areas of the indoor classroom – craft books in the creative area, cookery books in the role play area, books for babies in the home corner and construction and reference books in the small world area. This is how to create a literate environment. If the children have a folder or special book, these should be stored in low units so that the children can take them out and look at them whenever they wish.

Dry sand

Sand indoors is almost as popular as outdoors but is usually contained in a much smaller unit. I often suggest keeping this sand dry with fewer resources available than outdoors. On the storage unit in the photograph above there is shadowing on the higher shelves and baskets on the bottom shelf. Staff should constantly review the environment, and the resources in the baskets can be changed if the levels of involvement drop or if a particular interest emerges. Usually the baskets contain natural resources – shells, stones, twigs, etc. – and cups, plates and cutlery. The shadowed resources are various sizes and shapes and there is also a balance and a sand wheel. "Less is more" in this case – a varied selection of items ensures the sand is used purposefully. It is also worth considering resources made of metal or china to add a new dimension to the play. It is easier to have these items indoors, rather than outdoors, where they might go rusty or get broken more easily.

Water

Water fascinates young children and it is a vital component of any early years setting. Indoors, the water play is limited by the need to avoid flooding the whole class! The water tray should be filled every day but the resources can be left on the shelf nearby for the children to select independently. There is a photograph of a shelving unit with water resources on p. 41 of this chapter. Useful resources include a few boats, various containers, scoops, a water wheel, and so on. As with the indoor sand area, I would also recommend having some trays, the contents of which can be changed if levels of involvement drop. As a starting point for these, I would suggest shells, twigs, stones, sponges, syringes, pipettes, plastic sea and fresh water creatures. The higher shelves can be shadowed and, as long as the play is purposeful, these items do not need to be changed. As with dry sand, china and metal resources could be included for use in the indoor water area. Tidying up onto "shadows" is also a game in itself.

Role play

Caversham Nursery
School, Reading

If you ask children in Key Stage Two or even Key Stage Three what they remember about pre-school, nursery or Reception, many of them will say "the home corner"! They have strong and fond memories of the "miniature" house and the serious play that went on there. It is a vital component of young children's play as they take on the roles of the adults that they see around them. They put themselves into the position of someone else, imagine what that person would say, feel and do, and then act accordingly. This is a powerful way **to develop empathy** which is defined as "identification with and understanding of another's situation, feelings, and motives". It is tempting for adults to create complex role play areas but the home corner is the most familiar and therefore most relevant to young children. Other interests will arise during the year and so it is a good idea to have another area, either indoors or outside, that can be used to create a "pop-up" doctors, vet, shop and so on. But the house should be kept permanently, both indoors and outside if possible. As with all areas, try to organise the area so that the children can tidy it easily. Therefore, limit the amount of resources, particularly indoors. So there should be two dolls (not 22!) and just four cups, and so on.

Again, use the levels of involvement to determine whether you have the provision right – too many resources and the children cannot organise them to play purposefully, too few resources and the children might not have enough to do. In either case the levels of involvement will be low. When the resources are appropriate, in their amount, variety and complexity, then involvement will be high. It is possible to have real or very realistic resources, but children will use anything to maintain the play, so a piece of Numicon will become a biscuit or a wooden block will be a mobile phone.

ICT

ICT covers a broad range of activities and equipment. I look first at the aspect of technology that is causing practitioners the most concern – screens – on PCs, tablets, phones, game consoles, and so on. As I have stated, we use levels of involvement to assess whether an activity is engaging and valuable for the children. A child can appear to be deeply involved when operating a game on a screen.

This is not Level 5 involvement.

This is not a "whole brain" experience.

However, recent brain scan research has shown that, in fact, when using screen technology, only a small part of the brain is "lit up", rather than the large areas that are lit up during other activities such as building a den or using a hammer and nails. The addictive nature of such devices has also been proven, which will come as no surprise to many who have watched children become more and more obsessed with screen-based activities. We must then question and re-evaluate their use in our settings.

When evaluating screens in a setting, we should also take into account the amount of time that children are spending looking at screens at home. When computers were first introduced to settings, many children did not have access to them elsewhere. However, every mobile phone is now a powerful computer and 18-month-old babies know how to access certain apps by touching screens. With so much exposure to ICT at home, this again must make us re-evaluate its use in our settings.

One other factor to consider is that, because of the increase in technology in the home, children are spending less time playing outdoors or with creative equipment (construction toys, art equipment, etc.). Therefore, it is even more important that educational settings offer the experiences that children are not getting at home. We need to increase the amount of outdoor, active, creative, independent play that is not available elsewhere. This is another reason to re-evaluate the use of screens.

The early learning goal for **Technology** states that, "Children recognise that a range of technology is used in places such as homes and schools. They select and use technology for particular purposes." This wider consideration of technology fits more comfortably within a play-based setting.

If you do have iPads, they can be used to take photographs and videos and to look up information on the internet (rather like an instant encyclopaedia). An interactive whiteboard can be used to show photographs from home, photographs taken at school, video clips of activities in the setting or from the internet. It can also be used with selected programs – for example, to develop drawing as it involves large movements.

Digital cameras are very useful in a setting and, as explained in Chapter 5, a few children could take a camera home each week. Children can then be involved in the processes of showing the pictures on a screen and selecting some to print. Once printed, a child can cut them out to stick in their "special book". Children also often take pictures to print as part of a book or story.

Other equipment can be used in numerous areas of a setting. For example, indoors there can be digital clocks, programmable toys, CD players, door release buttons and a variety of role play equipment that requires technology such as microwaves, televisions, kettles, toasters, cash registers, remote controls, mobile phones, irons, calculators, digital scales, and so on. Outdoors the cameras can still be used, as can the CD player, metal detectors, walkie talkies, telephones and further role play equipment.

The single piece of equipment that I would suggest removing from classrooms is PCs. Staff often report problems caused by PCs (in terms of supervision, arguments, obsessive behaviours) and I do not feel these are outweighed by the benefits. The interactive whiteboard and iPads can be used in the same way but are far easier to remove, or switch off and iPads, in particular, are more versatile in their use.

In summary, any area or resource can be evaluated by assessing the levels of involvement that the children display. Children display the highest levels of involvement when they

ACTION PLAN

Use levels of involvement to monitor your environment and the resources.

Ensure outdoors is available for the maximum amount of time.

Read this chapter and organise a workshop-style environment.

Remember resources should be: accessible, versatile, authentic.

"Less is more" is a good phrase to keep in mind.

have autonomy, when they are pursuing their own interests in an environment that allows them to be creative, take risks and challenge themselves in their endeavours. The physical environment needs to be well laid out and equipped with high quality, open-ended, varied and authentic resources. As Sugata Mitra says: "Children learn to do what children want to learn to do" so let us support them by creating a superb enabling environment.

> We began putting *Planning in the Moment* into action in September 2016 after some considerable time getting our environment right. At the end of our first year I can see how it has benefitted both staff and the children in our care. The staff are now much less stressed, more relaxed and are free to spend quality time with the children, ensuring that no teachable moment is missed. They have all commented on how much better they feel they know their key children. The children's personal, emotional and social development has surpassed that of previous cohorts. They are much more resilient, independent, and show an excitement for learning, safe in the knowledge that the adults will follow their lead.

Nikki Smith, Manager, Little Learners Pre-school (pack-away setting), **2017**

> Ideally, may not the child learn to read and write when he feels ready for it? And by the method that seems to suit him best? Some seem to need picture and phonetic help, others take naturally to the written symbols and become rapid eye-readers.

Dora Russell, *In Defence of Children*, Hamish Hamilton, London, **1932**

Having used "in the moment planning" all year we have seen fantastic results. The children have amazed us this year with their independence, desire to learn and ability to reflect on their own learning. Our GLD is the highest it has ever been but more importantly the children are happy, engaged and truly involved and excited by their own learning.

Our areas that have made the biggest impact on our children have definitely been our sewing, art and woodwork areas. The children demonstrate such independent thinking in these areas. By allowing them to think for themselves and giving them access to everything they need, it enables them to create art, sewing and woodwork which is truly unique. They produce far better creations than when we used to ask them to make something specific as they have ownership over their own learning. These areas promote a huge amount of collaboration and development of children's language as they describe what they are making and support others who ask for help to create a similar product. We have loved seeing this collaboration and the pride with which children share their work is heart-warming. Another amazing part of these areas is the perseverance and patience that the children have shown. Often children will start a product then return to it the next day and sometimes even continue for weeks until they are satisfied with their work.

The introduction of our cooking area has been amazing! We have loved watching the children as they have become confident at making cakes independently with their peers. They relish the responsibility and trust that we allow them and rise to the challenge. This has massively impacted on their ability to negotiate with each other. We encourage the children to work independently from start to finish, just stepping in when they need the occasional support or when we see a teachable moment. Our cooking area has evolved over the year to add challenge to those who need it. We have introduced biscuit-making, where instead of balancing the ingredients they use teaspoons and tablespoons of each ingredient. Through this we have encouraged accurate counting and shown the children how to use a whiteboard to tally to help their friends. The biscuits help them with both their fine and gross motor skills as they stir, knead, roll and cut. After cooking the biscuits or cakes the children make icing if they want to and decorate them with sprinkles and toppings. They are encouraged to share equally between them and place in sandwich bags. Each product lends itself to a range of maths skills. Biscuits and cupcakes mean the children have to divide between the number of children who have cooked. Dividing a large cake means all our children understand halves, quarters and thirds.

Our journey to fully implement ITMP has been wondrous. I can't thank Anna enough for giving us the confidence to teach in a way we love. It has been a leap of faith for everyone but has been totally worth it and I would recommend it to anyone.

Suzi Strutt, Early Years Team Leader and Reception teacher, Thorley Hill Primary School, Bishop's Stortford, **2017**

4 The adult role

So far in this book, I have explained that **deep-level involvement indicates brain activity** and progress. Deep involvement will not occur unless a child has good levels of **well-being** and therefore this must be the priority. This means a focus on building relationships and meticulous planning of transitions and induction. Once a child is "settled", feels secure and trusts the adults, then his/her innate desire to learn can emerge. The best levels of involvement are then seen when children are allowed to initiate their own play. Therefore, I recommend arranging your settings to **maximise the amount of child-initiated play** (including access to outdoors) – if possible for the whole session. Where interruptions are essential, then ensure these are at the beginning or end of a session and that they are appropriate for the developmental stage of the children. **Clear boundaries and expectations are essential** so that children understand that the adults are in charge and they can relax and "be the children" within the given boundaries. Another essential element to high-quality child-initiated play is an **enabling environment** and Chapter 3 deals in detail with how this can be delivered to maximise engagement. Once we trust that children are hard-wired to learn, that we have ensured their well-being, that rules are clear and consistently applied, that they have long periods of time to play and that there is a superb environment, then the levels of involvement will leap. Children will become engaged, and purposeful in their play – demonstrating "concentration, creativity, energy and persistence" – all the signals of Level 5 involvement. Children, whatever age, want to be in this state, want to be engaged, want to be learning and do not want to be bored.

When everything is in place, as has been described so far, you will see children who are at Level 5 involvement, meaning that they are making progress. Most of these children will not be near an adult. Obviously this is not the case with babies but even the youngest baby will be deeply involved and content on their own for periods of time – figuring out how their hands move, how they make sounds with their mouth, how to hold on to that toy, trying to see what is in that watering can, etc. They do not always need adults with them in order to be learning.

In settings where there are older children and fewer adults, it is essential to recognise that the children are learning at all times, even when they are not with an adult. Indeed, some of the most powerful learning happens when the children are working things out for themselves, struggling to master a new skill, co-operating in a group or consolidating previous learning by practising something over and over. Settings need to be organised as described to ensure that most children are engaged independently of the adults. This means that they are learning at all times, engaged at all times and progressing at all times. Scan your setting and check that the children are indeed deeply involved, whether with an adult or not. This is a sure sign that your setting is working.

The best practitioner

What, then, are the adults supposed to be doing while the children are playing? In order to answer this question, I describe how the best practitioner operates and this will give readers a chance to reflect upon their own practice.

Go to the children, to their level, be interested and relaxed

The adult goes to the children. They do not call the children to them. The children are pursuing their own interests and are deeply involved in their play. The best adult will **scan the area** and decide where they think they are most needed or could be of most benefit. It is critical that the adult goes to where the children are engaged and interested because they are already invested in the play, challenging themselves, interested and keen to take the play further. Thus, there might be an opportunity for the adult to add something to the situation. In addition, by scanning, the adult will notice if any children are not engaged and can then assess the situation to decide if this is just a transition moment (when a child has finished one activity and is just about to move into another) or if the child does indeed need support of some kind to return to deep-level involvement.

The adult goes to the child's level. It is essential to crouch down or kneel so that your face is at the same height as that of the child. Early years practitioners have an exhausting job – getting up and down from the floor all day is just another thing that they do constantly.

The adult is interested, open, relaxed and smiling. The most vulnerable children are experts at reading the body language of adults. They may have had to learn to do so at home in order to stay safe. However, all children learn which adults they can trust, which ones are "a bit moody" or which ones shout a lot or are not really interested in their play. It is interesting to watch a setting and to note which adults are accepted into the play more than others. Children are quite astute at "reading" adults and will engage with those whom they can trust and who are genuinely interested in them.

Listen, watch and wait

The adult listens, watches and waits . . . and waits . . . and waits. This is probably the piece of advice I give to practitioners more than any other. "Just be quiet and wait." Waiting seems to be very difficult for a lot of practitioners, but it is the key when working with the youngest children.

Little Explorers, Thornton, Lancashire

The adult's voice will be quiet and calm.

While adults wait, they are PLANNING

While the adult is waiting, they are PLANNING how, *or if,* to respond. The best practitioner will be observing the children and thinking about what they see and hear. This means they are assessing. From this they will decide how to proceed – this is planning. At this point, it might be decided that the group, or child, is deeply involved in their play, making superb progress and that they, the adult, cannot actually add anything useful to this particular situation. At this point then **the adult might decide to move away**. It is very easy to spoil a child's play and sometimes it is better to leave them and move away. There will always be other children who will benefit from the adult attention.

The child leads the interaction

Once the adult finds a child or a group which they do want to interact with **the adult will let the child initiate the interaction**. If the child initiates the interaction, then the adult can be assured that it is the child's agenda, that the subject is something they are interested in and something that they are invested in. Quite often **the child will ask a question**. This is so much better than situations (which I see all too often) in which the adults are constantly asking questions. **The best practitioner will be *answering questions*, rather than asking them.**

The adult responds as appropriate

The adult will then respond as appropriate. Adults who work with young children know them "inside out" as unique individuals. The adults are therefore able to tailor their response to the particular child, in the particular situation, at that particular moment. They can spot the unique **"teachable moment"**. This is the ultimate in differentiation.

  The adult will respond in a way that will help the child to make progress. In other words, the adult will teach. There are many things that a practitioner can do in order to help a child to learn. They could be

> "communicating and modelling language, showing, explaining, demonstrating, exploring ideas, encouraging, questioning, recalling, providing a narrative for what they are doing, facilitating and setting challenges".

This quote comes from the current Ofsted inspection handbook and can be very useful in supporting practitioners to think carefully about how they respond to children in their setting. This is actually part of their definition of **teaching in the early years**.

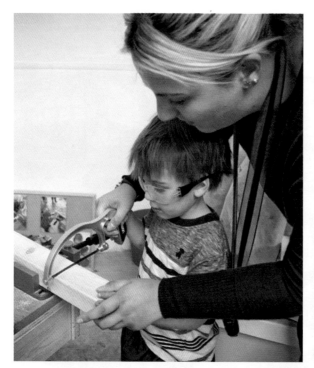

Try pondering

The adult will ponder if they want to find out something. By saying "**I wonder how . . .**" or "**I wonder** why . . .", a practitioner is saying to the child "I don't know the answer to this, but I am really interested and I am thinking about it." This allows the child time to respond if they wish, tells the child that the adult is genuinely interested and that the adult does not know everything, and encourages the child to think. It is far better than asking "What are you doing?" or "What shape is that?" Closed questions such as this do not add anything to the situation, rather the adult is just "testing" what the child already knows.

The adult will reflect on the impact they have made. If the adult has responded in an appropriate way, then the child will have made a step of progress (sometimes a very tiny step). In the best settings, the adults are constantly interacting with the children and moving their learning on in tiny steps, without disrupting the powerful vehicle which is their child-initiated play. To support this reflection, it is helpful for staff to consider "What would have happened if I had not been here?" This helps them to realise how much impact they are making. Over time, the progress of the cohort of children in such settings is outstanding. This is because as many "teachable moments" as possible are spotted and exploited by the staff.

The adult is constantly observing, waiting and responding. They are not writing. In many settings that I visit, the adults are often writing on post-its or clip boards or typing notes into a tablet. Writing up observations, whether onto paper or electronically, does not impact on the children. It is interacting with (i.e. teaching) children that will have an impact. Although there is a need to have evidence of what a child can do, the vast majority of this evidence will be in a practitioner's head and does not have to be documented, either on paper or electronically. Most settings do keep a certain amount of evidence in a child's "special book", "profile" or "learning journey". Such documents have numerous names, but there is a tendency for the recording of this evidence to take

over as the main role of a practitioner. This is a mistake. Practitioners need to be observing and immediately interacting with the children in their setting, not just writing down what they see happening.

Focus on prime areas for younger children

If working with children in the early years, then the prime areas must take priority. In particular, as explained in Chapter 1, many children are missing out on vital interactions in the home and therefore we are seeing more language delay, poor social skills and delays in physical development. With a decrease in the number of speech therapists, the promotion of speech and language is becoming a key part of the work of early years practitioners. Many interactions will focus on this area of learning. Staff are not able to wait for a child to receive help from speech therapy sessions. Rather, they need to become skilled in this themselves. Some simple strategies can be employed to support language development within child-initiated play sessions.

Strategies for language development

If an adult spots a teachable moment when they can **enhance language development**, there are **numerous specific strategies that can be used**:

a. **An adult reflects back** what the child has said (having waited for the child to speak first!) to ensure they have understood correctly. So, for example, Zara says, "baby eat", and the adult responds, "The baby is eating?"

b. This response from the adult also then includes **scaffolding and modelling** – adding extra words to the phrase and modelling correct sentence structure.

c. In this case, because the child is at an early stage of development in spoken English, the adult should accompany the verbal response with the use of **Makaton**. This is a signing system that should be introduced to **all** children and which particularly supports communication for children with English as an additional language, children who are shy and children with language delay, but also then allows every child to communicate with every other child in the setting.

d. The response is also **tailored to the unique child**. The adults need to know the children very well in order to ensure that their response is appropriate – giving the child the correct amount of new learning – not too much and not too little. In this case the adult knew that Zara was sometimes using the article "the" and so reminded her of this and also introduced the word "is" as new learning. For another child in the class, the adult response might well have been different because they would have assessed and responded according to their knowledge of *that child*.

e. Staff should **avoid too many questions** (remembering that questions can be stressful and that we want to avoid stress for the children), but should do a lot of **pondering**. For example, Jaden says, "Look! The ball went on the roof." And the adult responds, "Oh, it is stuck so high up. **I wonder** how we can get it down." The response has involved reflecting back, scaffolding, modelling and pondering – all tailored to this particular child. In this way, the adult **invites but does not insist on further communication**.

f. For a child who is more reticent to speak, an adult can sometimes **commentate** as the child plays – again tailored to the particular child. For example, the adult might say "Oh you have made five sausages to fry in the pan." The child will be hearing the language and might use it later when the adult is not there.

g. Sometimes the interaction will involve some **direct teaching**. For example, Arda says, "I want this." (*He points to the nail in another child's woodwork model.*) The adult responds, "This is called a 'nail'. Can you say that? . . . 'Nail'." Arda responds, "Nail. I want a nail." The adult uses the Makaton sign for "please" to prompt Arda and he then says, "I want a nail, please."

Practitioners in the early years have approximately 1,000 interactions per day. In the best settings, each of these interactions is a cycle in which the adult observes something, assesses it and responds appropriately in order to move the learning on – i.e. they plan and teach **in a matter of moments**. This means that each day a practitioner has 1,000 interactions leading to 1,000 tiny steps of development, all adding up and resulting in outstanding progress over time. The practitioners are **planning in the moment** 1,000 times per day.

However, if a practitioner were to record each interaction after it had been completed, then they would not have anywhere near 1,000 interactions, but would probably have approximately 100 or less. Therefore, we have a choice to make. Are we going to have 1,000 interactions per day and teach 1,000 next steps, with just a small amount of documented evidence, or are we going to try and document everything that happens, thereby reducing the number of interactions to less than 100 (meaning also that less than 100 next steps have been taught)? The choice is very simple. **Let's write less and interact more**.

Chapter 5 suggests a way in which to keep adequate amounts of documented evidence, which is unique to each child, valued by them and their family, but which does not overwhelm staff. However, **the most important role of the adult is to observe, assess, plan and teach – all in a matter of moments**.

ACTION PLAN

Ask staff to describe the "perfect practitioner".

Video some staff interacting with children.

Use this chapter to reflect on the videos and how to improve the interactions.

Make sure staff <u>watch and wait</u> before interacting.

Ask practitioners "What would have happened if you hadn't been there?"

Try to reduce the number of questions that adults ask children.

Use the Ofsted definition of teaching to give ideas of "teaching" strategies that staff can use – modelling, suggesting, etc.

I will be the first to admit our room was not exactly how I wanted it to be this term but by moving a few tables around and creating more open shelving we were able to see how the children were accessing equipment and using the areas. At first, they were a bit surprised that nothing was set out for them but as the term has progressed they have become very good at deciding what they would like to learn and where. I noticed a change in the way they talk about learning in the class; instead of asking "What are we learning about today?", there is more " Can we find out about. . .? " and "I would like to try. . .".

The topics are not pre-planned but come naturally from the children's interests and our observations and our commitment to "go with it" and develop these ideas. This system allowed us to have in-depth conversations each day about individual children. We were able to immediately see their interests, lines of development and next steps. For example, Serhat has pursued his interest in numbers by making maps with numbered houses, a list of numbers counting in twos up to 400 and, his latest project, the number book. He has continued this over a week and is proud that he is now up to 800 and is determined to have at least 40 pages in the book.

Ella Richardson and **Lauren Davies**, Reception teachers,
Brindishe Green Primary School, Lewisham, **2017**

It is cruel to say "Don't touch!" It simply means "Don't learn, don't grow, don't be intelligent."

Susan Isaacs, *The Nursery Years*, Routledge & Kegan Paul, London, **1929**

5 The paperwork

Many readers will have turned to this chapter without reading the rest of the book. My plea is that you go back and read the earlier chapters first. The paperwork that accompanies the best early years practice is the least important part of that practice. An understanding of brain development will give you the confidence to explain why child-initiated play, above all else, is the best way for children to learn. Chapter 1 explains that child-initiated play leads to deep levels of involvement, indicating brain development and progress. To organise a setting which ensures that as many children as possible are displaying this deep level of involvement is a hugely complex task. Chapter 2 looks at how the routines (or timetables), expectations and "rules" have to be established and maintained because it is within this framework that young children will relax, feel secure and be able to explore, become engaged and learn. Chapter 3 explores the critical factors that create an enabling environment. Without a superb environment, it is very difficult to have all children engaged and learning through child-initiated play. Chapter 4 considers another critical factor – the role of the adults within child-initiated play (which is to observe, assess, plan and teach **in a**

matter of moments). This has recently become known as **planning in the moment** but, as stated in the Introduction, **this is nothing new**; it is just good practice.

This chapter describes the paperwork that has been developed as a way of recording some of the teaching cycles that occur thousands of times each day in a setting where children are initiating their own play. However, I stress again that this chapter alone, explaining a new format for paperwork, will not improve your practice. It is the practice that has to change first and then the paperwork that supports the practice can be re-examined.

This book has explained why child-initiated play is so valuable and I am advocating that this is what children should be doing for most, if not all, of their time in a setting. If possible, they should **never** be called away from their play during a session. They should not be doing focussed activities, subject-specific lessons, assemblies, interventions, group times, snack time or (in school) play time. They do not need to be told what, where or how to play. Within the given rules and boundaries, they should have the **freedom to learn** in a way that suits them and about the things that interest them. If children have genuine choice, then it is impossible to predict what they are going to choose to do and therefore it is impossible (and a waste of time) to try and pre-plan what they will do. The adult's role is purely to observe the play, assess what they see, plan how to respond and then teach next steps immediately in a way that is uniquely suited to the particular child in that particular moment.

Each adult will be doing this hundreds of times each day. It is not necessary, or desirable, to record all such teaching cycles and the remainder of this chapter describes a tried-and-tested model for recording a sample of these cycles. The sample is sufficient to meet all legal requirements, and enough in terms of documented evidence about a child but, more importantly, it is enough to keep parents informed and involved and to give the children a unique record of their time in a setting.

In the simplest terms, the children are all initiating their own play and the adults are interacting with all the children, teaching next steps as often as possible. Each week the adults will select a few children to be the "focus children" and will record some of the interactions that they have with these focus children. If there is a child in your setting who has one-to-one support, I would recommend that he/she is, in fact, a "focus child" every week. This ensures that you have a record of how the extra support for that child is being deployed and what impact it is having on the child.

Focus children and parental involvement

Each week, usually on a Friday, staff select the "focus children" for the following week. This is ten per cent of the group – so in a Reception or Year One class this is three children, and in a nursery of 26 children, it would also be approximately three children each week. In a room for younger children aged two and three, staff might select 20 per cent of the group to be the focus children as they have higher staff ratios and the children make progress more rapidly. With babies, and for childminders, perhaps one in four could be the focus. In settings where children do varying amounts of hours and sessions, then decide for yourself what is a manageable amount. Do not start with too many children as it will take time to get used to the recording of interactions, and it is easier to focus on just a few children at a time. I would not advise choosing one child from each key person (except in a baby room). In fact, it is better to select all the focus children from one key person and then all staff will get to know those children. If you choose ten per cent, then each child will be a focus child once per term. If you choose 20 per cent (for children aged two and three), then they will be a focus child each half term. In a baby room and as a childminder, you could end up with each child being a focus every four weeks. At the beginning of the year I recommend that you choose children who have settled quickly, show good levels of involvement and appear quite confident. There are many reasons for this: they will be able to cope with some close attention; they are confident enough for staff to give them some appropriate challenges; also, their Learning Journey sheet (see details below) will be completed quite quickly – this is important at this early stage of the year, because the staff still have to work hard with the settling of many of the other children.

When the children have been selected they are given a parent consultation sheet to take home (see Appendix E) and also a digital camera. In settings where an on-line learning journal is used, the parents of the focus children could be asked to upload some photographs from home. If cameras are not available to send home, parents could be asked to email some pictures from their phone. Staff should speak to parents and explain that the family should fill in the sheet in as much detail as possible and also take some photographs over the weekend. Because you are only trying to get a few parents each week to complete these sheets, it is possible to approach them individually and remind them. Some parents might want someone to scribe their responses for them and staff will know which families this is likely to apply to. I would recommend that you create your own sheets for your parents. There are two examples of completed parent sheets below.

Carterhatch

Infant School • Children's Centres

Planning for your child's learning journey

Next week we will be focusing on ___Deshna___ _28/10/13_ We will be observing them while they play to find out more about their interests and how they are progressing. Please take some pictures (**no more than 15**) of your child/family enjoying activities out of school.

We value the knowledge and understanding you have of your child and would really appreciate it if you would share this with us so that together we can plan activities to meet your child's needs. This will help us plan for their future learning and development.

Is there anything significant happening in your child's life at the moment e.g. visits, holidays, new pets, family celebrations? Is there anything you would like to tell us about your child?

We will be celebrating Diwali (The festival of lights) on Sunday 03 November. On this occasion we pray to the God & Goddesses, make lots of sweets & savories, We dress in new clothes, visit friends & families & distribute sweets. On celebration ends with the lighting of candles, diyas, fire crackers.
Deshna is very fond of cooking, she likes to help in the kitchen. She also likes music & dancing. She is also keen to learn numbers, alphabets & nursery rhymes.

Do you have anything you would like to ask us about your child's progress and development in Nursery?

We would like to know about the different activities she does at school & how she communicates with her teachers and friends.

Please return this sheet with the school camera by Monday 28 Oct so that we can add your thoughts and ideas to the planning process. Please ensure that the camera is used with adult supervision, kept away from water and no objects are places on the cameras LED screen. Thank you, Butterfly class staff

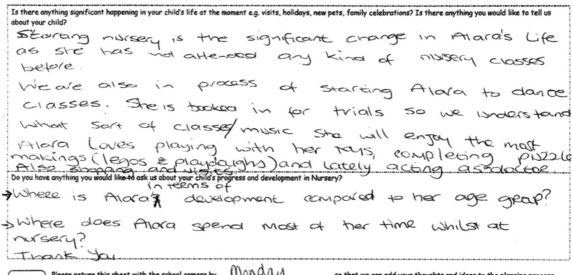

Both the consultation sheet and camera are returned after the weekend or the photographs are uploaded or emailed into the setting. The information provided by the parents is fascinating and staff often find out about events that the child might never have revealed such as visiting relatives, family events, new pets, and so on. The completed sheets can be stored in the child's folder or special book or photographed and stored electronically – a lovely example of the parents' voice. The photographs will often link to this information

and can prompt the child to talk about these things. A colleague who introduced cameras in her nursery was delighted when a girl brought the camera back with photographs of two pigs which were living in her garden! This child had never spoken in nursery, but the genuine fascination of the staff, and the child's expert knowledge of pigs, meant that she felt able to talk about them. Once her confidence was boosted by this event, she carried on speaking regularly in nursery. In my experience, many of the photographs show children getting involved with cooking at home, spending time at the shops and with relatives.

It is possible to print some photographs from each child to put in their folder or special book and note down anything that the child says about the pictures. For children aged three and older, some of the photographs can be shown on the interactive whiteboard or on a laptop as the year progresses and the group settles, allowing other children in the group to see the pictures. If they are able, the child can be encouraged to talk about the photographs as they are shown and an adult can write down exactly what they say.

Photographs from home can be printed. Even very young children will point to these pictures and be thrilled to see faces that they recognise from home.

Planning in the moment for individual children – Learning Journey sheets

On Monday one Learning Journey sheet is put up on the planning board for each of the focus children (see Appendices F, G and H). I would advise you to create your own sheet and adapt it to suit your setting. As seen in the Appendices, the sheets vary according to the age of the child. For example, with children under three years old I only want to track the prime areas and therefore the sheet is much simpler. In Year One the curriculum is broken down into subjects and therefore the sheet looks different again. On each sheet (apart from that for the under threes) there is a box in which staff can tick off various areas of learning as they are covered. When developing this paperwork, we included this box as a way of reassuring ourselves that this system would deliver full coverage of all areas of learning. In fact, since starting this system ten years ago, I have never had a box that was not ticked. If you find that you are not getting coverage of certain areas, then look at your environment and the opportunities it offers. Try to introduce areas of the environment or resources that will support this coverage and also ensure that staff are thinking holistically in their interactions, rather than in a narrow way.

The Learning Journey sheets are blank at the start of the week, except for the name, date and some notes to remind staff about any particular areas that they wish to focus on with this child and anything that the parents have asked about. There are several examples of completed Learning Journey sheets, for children of various ages, at the end of this chapter.

The Introduction explains the theory behind this approach. In brief, an enabling environment needs to be set up that is the best possible and then the children allowed to learn by initiating their own play. The staff observe and interact with the children in their pursuits – looking out for "teachable moments" in which they can make a difference. Some of these interactions with the focus children are then recorded on the Learning Journey sheets. All adults, who interact with a focus child, contribute to the Learning Journeys. This process contains a moment in which the adult has to "plan" what to do as a result of what he/she has observed.

In many settings, observations are made, the plans are written down and the activity is delivered at a later date. With the system that I am advocating, staff do not do any such forward planning – rather they remain "in the moment" with the child and respond immediately. If a child is concentrating on using a hammer at two p.m. on Monday, this is the moment in which a skilful adult can interact with the child and "teach" them how to use the hammer effectively. The child is motivated and interested in that moment and therefore keen to learn. Such an interaction might appear on a Learning Journey as follows ("T" indicates "adult" [childminders prefer to use "I"]). Note that the record of the interaction includes the observation, the teaching and the outcome:

> *Alara was trying to hammer in a nail but it kept falling over. "T" modelled how to hold the nail between thumb and finger and tap gently. Alara watched carefully and then copied the technique correctly. The nail stayed upright and Alara was then able to hammer it firmly.*

Highlight the "teaching" (I usually use yellow). **It is vital that entries on Learning Journeys contain an element of teaching.** Some observations, without any "plan" or "teaching" can also be recorded but not included on the Learning Journeys – rather they are stored separately in the child's individual folder. These are usually referred to as "Wow!" moments. But the entries on the Learning Journeys are intended to be a record of some planning and teaching. Therefore, they are interactions when an adult has been involved and has had some impact on the child, teaching a next step in that moment.

Another example might read:

> *Nadir was struggling to cut a piece of tape. "T" modelled how to use the dispenser and explained about the blade. Nadir persevered to try and cut the tape. "T" praised his efforts and encouraged him to keep trying. Eventually Nadir was delighted to cut a piece of tape himself.*

I visit many settings and often see plans for focussed activities or circle times related to the teaching of sharing and turn-taking. However, it is far more powerful to do this teaching at a moment when it is relevant to the children in a real situation. For example an entry on Kai's Learning Journey reads:

> *Kai wanted a go on the bike. "T" modelled the phrase and Kai repeated "Can I have a turn please?" "T" encouraged Kai to say this to the boy on the bike. Kai did so and the boy gave the bike to Kai. The two boys then took turns independently.*

The focus for the youngest children will be almost exclusively around the prime areas of personal, social and emotional development, physical development and communication and language. For example, for a two-month-old baby with a childminder, an entry on the Learning Journey reads:

> *"Sophie was waving her arms and looking animated. I modelled speech, saying 'I wonder what you are going to say, Sophie.' I waited and Sophie made a loud shouting noise and smiled."*

In the case of two year olds, language and socials skills are often the main subject of the teaching:

> *Toby is trying to take playdough from Kaan. "T" models the phrase, "Can I have some please?" and Toby copies saying "un sum pease"? Kaan hands over some playdough. "T" reminds Toby to say "Thank you", Toby says "ank oo".*

In this example, the practitioner has written exactly what the child said and this becomes evidence of this child's language ability on that particular day. It is a good idea to highlight the child's words in a different colour.

For older children, the focus of the teaching might be very different, but the teaching cycle is the same. For example, in Year One:

> *Jamie has completed his story about batman but has not added any full stops. "T" reminds him about the full stops. "T" encourages Jamie to read through his story to see where the full stops need to go. Jamie reads his story and successfully adds the full stops.*

In all these examples, the children made progress in a very short space of time. Whenever anyone is observing child-initiated play (possibly from the local authority, Ofsted or a senior leader), it is important to have a member of the staff team with them in order to point out the progress being made and the "teaching" that enabled the progress to happen. I am often asked about "next steps" and how these are noted/remembered. I point out that when working "in the moment", **the next steps are carried out immediately** and therefore do not need to be recorded anywhere else. I have visited many settings where practitioners have written down hundreds of next steps and the staff are stressed trying to remember them all and trying to find time to teach them!

The diagram below shows the traditional teaching cycle that is recognised as best practice. The timescale for the duration of the cycle is where "in the moment" practice differs from many settings. The whole cycle is completed hundreds of times each day (some of which are recorded), whereas in many settings the cycle is spread over a day or a week, with observations happening on one day and the resulting activity happening the next day or the next week.

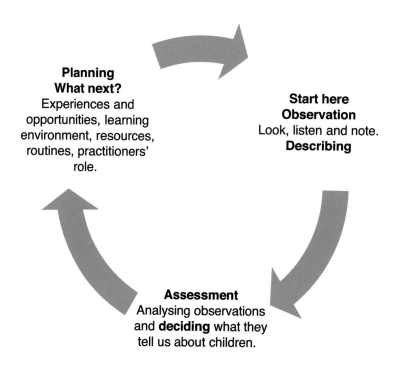

Planning
What next?
Experiences and opportunities, learning environment, resources, routines, practitioners' role.

Start here
Observation
Look, listen and note.
Describing

Assessment
Analysing observations and **deciding** what they tell us about children.

However, it is recognised that to respond immediately is the most powerful way to teach our youngest children. The National Strategies document *Learning, Playing and Interacting* states that:

> Babies and young children . . . are experiencing and learning in the here and now, not storing up their questions until tomorrow or next week. It is in that moment of curiosity, puzzlement, effort or interest – the "teachable moment" – that the skilful adult makes a difference. By using this cycle on a moment-by-moment basis, the adult will be always alert to individual children (observation), always thinking about what it tells us about the child's thinking (assessment), and always ready to respond by using appropriate strategies at the right moment to support children's well-being and learning (planning for the next moment).
>
> National Strategies, *Learning, Playing and Interacting*, DfE 2009, p. 23

This is exactly what I suggest adults should do throughout every session in their setting. The schedule for inspectors has a useful quote too:

> Teaching should not be taken to imply a "top down" or formal way of working. It is a broad term which covers the many different ways in which adults

help young children learn. It includes their interactions with children during planned and child-initiated play and activities: communicating and modelling language, showing, explaining, demonstrating, exploring ideas, encouraging, questioning, recalling, providing a narrative for what they are doing, facilitating and setting challenges.

Ofsted Inspection Handbook, September 2015

These are exactly the kind of things which I suggest staff should record on the Learning Journeys. The quote above from Ofsted is included in Appendix I and I suggest it is put on the wall beside the Learning Journey sheets to support staff in completing entries on them. Staff can then reflect upon their role: Did I model? Did I demonstrate something? Did I provide a resource? Did I scaffold? and so on. A good tip for staff members is for them to ask themselves: "What would have happened if I hadn't been here?" The impact that the adult has had then becomes more obvious.

Staff often take a photograph of the events and these can also be added to the Learning Journey. By the end of the week, the sheet is full of notes and photographs – a unique record of the child's learning and development during that week. Several examples of completed sheets are shown later in the book and these cover children from the age of seven months to children in Year One. Teachers who have tried this way of working report that they are not only re-inspired and happy in their role but have also got to know the children in far more depth and as unique individuals.

The key person or teacher should keep a colour copy of each Learning Journey in their planning file, the original copy can go in the child's folder and a copy should also be given to parents. Again, if using an on-line system it is possible to complete a paper Learning Journey and then take a photograph of this to upload to the child's on-line profile.

Once the Learning Journey sheet is complete, the parents of the child can be invited into your setting for a discussion about the week and all that you have learnt about the child. Any points the parents have written on the consultation form can be discussed and parents encouraged to add comments to the child's folder. Together you can agree on possible areas for focus in future and give the parents some ideas of things to be doing at home to support these areas. This means that in Reception, for example, the teacher will have three parent meetings each week, rather than the nightmare of the usual parents' evenings. These weekly meetings are so much easier and meaningful. You have the Learning Journey to discuss and, as you have spent the week focussing on the child that you are discussing, your knowledge and understanding of that child is deep and accurate.

I stress again that, although they do give the focus children a bit more attention, the staff are interacting with *all* the children, but do not record all interactions – they only record some of their interactions with the focus children on their learning journeys. The focus child system ensures that every child gets some records created every term (or half term for children under three years old). It also ensures that the "invisible child" becomes visible as staff seek them out during their focus week, eager to find out what the child is doing and how they can support the child to develop. Without a systematic way of keeping records it is easy to slip back into the situation where you are recording far too much, as interesting things are happening constantly. The system also avoids a situation in which there is far more documentation for a child that is always eager and ready to show you something and is demanding your attention. The focus child system means that, although not everything is recorded, you still have records of learning for each child each term (or half term).

Planning in the moment for groups of children – Group sheets

What about the rest of the group if we are only focussing on a few children? This is a question I am asked over and over. The answer is simple. The other children carry on with their own learning and **adults are interacting with all the children and teaching them too**. However, such interactions are not written down. Sometimes children are playing and learning on their own, sometimes with a friend or a group and sometimes by joining an activity with one of the focus children. The adults have time for everyone. They are not totally absorbed with the focus children – this would be overwhelming for those children. The adults are often free to support other individuals or groups. If working in a setting **with children aged three and older**, you will notice that they often play in groups or, when one child starts to do something, others want to join in.

When this system was first developed ten years ago, we decided that we wanted a record of some of these group activities. Therefore, we developed a separate A3 sheet on which to record activities involving a group (see Appendix J). Again, this can be started on a Monday and completed during the week. You may end up with three or four of these sheets by the end of the week. The sheet is again designed to record the whole teaching cycle: observation – assessment and plan – teaching – outcome. Examples of completed sheets are shown later in this chapter. Staff should review this sheet and amend it according to the needs of the setting. I would not recommend including children's names on these sheets – they are a record of a group activity when an adult has been involved and had an impact. If an individual child has learnt something from the activity, then they will demonstrate this at a later date and this can then be recorded as evidence of attainment – a "Wow!" moment for that individual child.

As with individual children, staff look out for activities or events that have captured the interest of a group. They will join the group to see if they can support, enhance or develop the activity in any way. Thus, they are observing and assessing. Sometimes the group operates independently and with deep-level involvement and any attempt to join the activity might actually disrupt it. In this situation, the adult may observe for a while, possibly taking particular note of some children, and then move away. However, on many occasions a skilful adult will spot a "teachable moment". They then decide what to do – this is planning. They might provide an extra resource, an idea, some vocabulary, some information, or they might model a skill or demonstrate how to use a piece of equipment – this is teaching. A few examples are shown in the grid opposite. **Remember – this Group sheet would not be useful for children aged under three years old**.

Observation and assessment	Plan and teaching	Outcome
Children attempting to build a tent by placing fabric on teepee frame. (Children are unaware of how to use pegs.)	"T" showed the children the box of pegs and modelled how to use them to secure the fabric in place.	The tent was then built by the group.
Children putting snails in the water tray (unaware or not caring about the snails).	"T" explains that snails cannot swim. "T" suggests making a new area where the snails could explore.	Children build an exciting environment for the snails and observe them moving around.
Children playing lively role play adventure in the garden.	"T" encourages them to re-tell the adventure. "T" models writing and scribes the story that the children tell.	The story is completed and acted out at group time at the end of the session.

The two photographs below are included to give readers an impression of what these two sheets look like when completed. For more detailed examples, please go to the end of this chapter.

Entries on both sheets should include

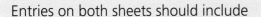

- Observation
- Teaching
- Outcome

Planning in the moment for an individual child

Planning in the moment for a group

"Wow!" moments

Within an enabling environment and with all this wonderful teaching, the children will soon start to do things independently and when such moments are observed they might be referred to as "Wow!" moments. Staff should write "snapshot" observations of these moments, but only when the child does something independently, for the first time. For example, "Jayden went to the toilet on his own and remembered to wash his hands" or, "Sasha said 'Help me please!' in a loud, clear voice." These observations might be accompanied by a photograph and should be dated and annotated to explain why they are noteworthy for a particular child. In settings that are using an on-line system, and in which staff are trying to work "in the moment", tablets are often just used for truly "Wow!" moments and the entries uploaded to the child's profile as evidence of attainment.

Content of folders/special books

In Chapter 6 it is stated clearly that there is no legal requirement to keep documented evidence of attainment. However, if you have read this book carefully, you will see that there are indeed various items that make up a child's special book or folder. These include the child's stories, their Learning Journey sheets, photographs from home, consultation sheets from parents, evidence of "Wow!" moments and anything that the child might want to keep in their folder. However, **each special book will be unique**, because each child will have had a unique experience within the setting.

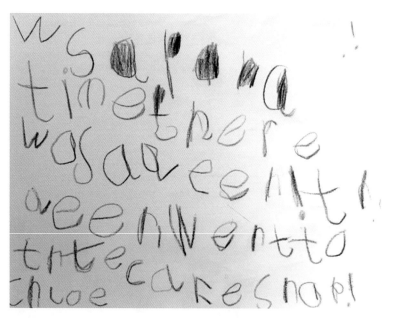

Richmond Avenue Primary School, Southend

Summary of planning in the moment

- The children are initiating their own play (for almost all their time in a setting) as this is when they are deeply involved (an indication of brain activity and progress).
- The adults do not know what the children will choose to do; therefore, they cannot plan ahead. The adults constantly observe, assess, plan and teach, completing this cycle hundreds of times each day.
- Each week a few children are chosen as the "focus children" for the week. Their parents are given a consultation form and, if possible, they will provide some photographs from home.
- The adults will record some "teaching cycles" or interactions on Learning Journey sheets for the "focus children" each week. (This is ten per cent of the group, or 20 per cent or 25 per cent for children under 36 months).
- The adults will also record some "teaching cycles" when they have been working with a group.
- Finally, any truly "Wow!" moments will be recorded for children when they are observed doing something independently for the first time.
- Once the Learning Journeys are completed for the focus children, their parents are invited into the setting for a meeting with a member of staff.

In Chapter 6, assessment and tracking is discussed. However, before examining this in detail, I would like to stress that:

- It is not necessary to "cross-reference" the entries on the Learning Journeys to developmental milestones or any kind of tracker.
- It is not necessary to spend time cross-referencing "Wow!" moments to any kind of tracker.
- Practitioners need to regain the confidence to recognise that the vast majority of evidence is in their heads.

The practice at Caldecote changed from quite structured, adult-led learning to a far greater emphasis on child-initiated play with "planning in the moment". Time and money was invested in both staff training and in the development of the environment – particularly outdoors. The children are now keen to come to school to play with their friends and teachers. They know that they will have fun learning with the activities and in the way that they choose. Following the children's interests means the children and adults are excited to find out what each new day will bring. It has also enabled all adults to get to know the children inside out. Not only are the teachers helping the children to learn, they are able to enjoy the time playing with the children who are highly motivated and following their own interests. The children and adults are deeply involved in meaningful conversations and interactions and clearly enjoying each other's company – a pleasure to see and be a part of. The impact on progress and attainment has been remarkable too, with the percentage of children gaining a good level of development rising from below 20 per cent to above 60 per cent over the four year period.

Laura Christy, Caldecote Primary School, Leicester, **2017**

I wanted to share a parent's perspective of "in the moment planning" (namely, my husband's!) as, whilst I have been using "in the moment planning" in my own setting we found out (much to my joy!) when my son started at nursery in September that they too were going to start "in the moment planning".

As my husband does the drop offs he has had two parent meetings so far. It has been lovely to see him so animated when talking about our son's learning and he has brought copies of the focus week sheets home to share. Both he and my son are really proud of them and they have been shown to various grandparents too! Some of the comments he has made have included "it's great as these stories with the pictures and the learning make sense now", "it's nice to see the variety of stuff he does over a week", "it's lovely to see how the teachers actually work with him", "they really seem to know him and how to make him shine", "I can't believe that he can remember how to make cakes on his own" (my mum's comment!).

The contrast for me is really clear (compared to our experience with our older daughter). My husband has felt really empowered by the whole experience – a true partner in supporting our son's learning at nursery. For me the hardest part of never doing pick ups or drop offs, due to my own job, has been softened by the fact that I, too, can contribute through the parental info sheet that is sent home and chat to our son about his focus weeks with him.

As for our son, he has thrived – his language development and confidence, especially, as he seems so engaged in whatever he is doing at nursery – and there is not a toilet roll penguin in sight!!! So, thank you Anna and all the wonderful practitioners using the "in the moment planning" and spreading the word! It has been the most wonderful start to our little boy's education and we are so grateful to everyone xxx.

Clare Peck, parent, teacher, member of Facebook group "Keeping Early Years Unique", **2017**

Don't call a thing "naughty" when you mean merely "it's a nuisance to me". . . .
Don't interrupt anything a child is doing without giving him fair warning. . . . Don't
"take" the child for a walk – go with him.

Susan Isaacs, *Advice for Parents*, Routledge & Kegan Paul, London, **1929**

Learning Journey for: Kara   Date: 17.4.17   Age: 7 months

Entries should include the initial observation (& assessment), the teaching and the outcome.

Current interests, patterns in learning or information from parents:

- Introduce meat into her diet.
- Continue to model Makaton signs: Up/ milk/ stop/ more/ finished.
- Develop crawling opportunities.

Kara discovered a musical toy. Kara became fascinated by the flashing light and revolving duck. **T** modelled how to press the buttons to change the music. Kara went on to play with this toy for over 10 minutes.

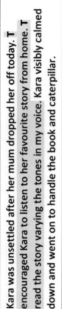

Kara lifted her body off of the ground and began to rock forwards and backwards. **T** placed several of Kara's toys at various points on the rug and encouraged Kara to crawl to them. Kara moved across the rug crawling and collapsing. She then spotted something more interesting than her toys, the TV controller! Kara then crawled quickly over to it. Continue to use this as a motivator.

Kara was unsettled after her mum dropped her off today. **T** encouraged Kara to listen to her favourite story from home. **T** read the story varying the tones in my voice. Kara visibly calmed down and went on to handle the book and caterpillar.

At lunch time **T** introduced a new puree for Kara to try which contained meat. Kara allowed me to feed her one spoon full before taking hold of the spoon and chewed it. **T** began feeding Kara with another spoon. Kara was happy to eat several spoonful's of the puree before turning her head away. **T** modelled the Makaton sign for *more* and *finish*. Kara responded to the finish sign. **T** went on to give Kara finger foods to try. Appeared to enjoy the cucumber.

Kara showed an interest in a pop up toy. She pulled out the pieces and began sucking them. **T** commented on what she was doing 'you have the blue person. Now you're putting him in your mouth'. Kara began to babble 'addda' **T** repeated back what she had said. Kara smiled and continued to engage with the conversation. **T** modelled other sounds such as m, g and u.

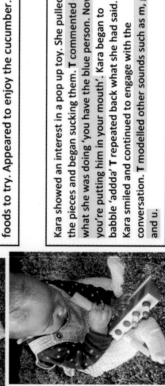

Possible Areas For Future Focus:

- Continue to develop Kara's interest in speaking and modelling new sounds.
- Continue to use Makaton signs: Up/ milk/ stop/ more/ finished.
- Develop crawling opportunities using motivators.
- Create opportunities to interact with peers.

Planning in the moment Learning Journey for a baby aged seven months with childminder (Please note, it is not necessary to type the Learning Journey)

Learning Journey For Hal .... Date 15-5-17   (15 months)

Entries should include the initial observation (& assessment), the teaching and the outcome.

Current interests, patterns in learning or information from parents
* Enjoying helping at home - dishwasher
* using several Makaton signs
* Positioning schema

Hal fascinated by large box of buttons & coins. He put one towards his mouth. (T) said 'no!' & reminded Hal not to eat coins. Hal picked up several coins & put them in his pockets. (T) suggested he put some in the till. Hal spent 20 mins moving from box to pocket to till and back again.

Hal tried to snatch a duplo plane from another child. (T) Modelled how to make a plane. Hal watched and tried to make one. (T) Modelled "help please" Hal did sign for "help". Making appropriate sound. (T) facilitated sharing. Hal played happily.

Hal was picking up stones & putting them down on other stone. (T) demonstrated how they looked different on that block paving. Hal played happily picking stones & placing on blocks.

Hal found a car and did sign for "more" (T) reminded him when can were. Hal spent 10 mins lining up and singing to himself.

Hal found piece of bark on path & picked it up. He found more pieces. (T) mirrored his play & then modelled making a slope on grass. Hal placed his pieces in a line & spent a long time looking for more pieces. (T) modelled "More" & Hal copied sign & said "mo", doing sign & ...

Hal picked up apple & went to walk away. (T) reminded him to sit & eat. Hal sat & ate the apple.

Possible Areas For Future Focus:
* Show Mum Makaton signs for 'help' & 'water'
* Mum to Hal to climb more
* Look out for Hal putting coins in his mouth

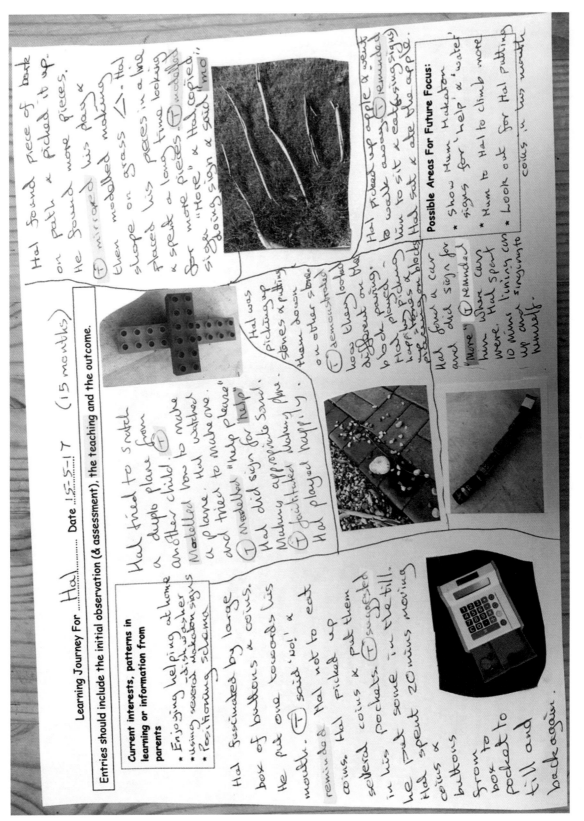

Planning in the moment Learning Journey for a baby aged 15 months in a private nursery

Learning Journey for: Noah   **Term** Spring 1

Current Next Steps:

From Parent/Carers:
To develop Noah's vocabulary and confidence in speaking

From Practitioners:
N/A as a first prime week.

Future Next Steps:

From Parent/Carers:

From Practitioners: To use Noah's interest of music to learn a small bout of songs.
To develop Noah's vocabulary and confidence in speaking

	Learning Journey	1	2	3	4	5
		✓				

30th Jan - 3rd February 2017

Areas	
Personal, Social & Emotional	✓✓✓✓
Physical	✓✓✓✓
Communication & Language	✓✓✓
Literacy	✓
Mathematics	
Understanding the World	
Expressive Arts & Design	
Characteristics	
Playing and Exploring	✓
Active Learning	✓
Creating and Thinking Critically	

1.2.17 HM- see photo
At "tidy-up" time, (T) asked Noah if he knew where the watering cans went. He didn't respond so (T) showed Noah where to put it. Noah found another watering can and seemed very pleased (T) asked Noah if he knew where a pot went, he excitedly responded saying "yes, there!" Noah continued to tidy away pots, pans and utensils. He pointed to show me. (T) responded "All in the basket." Noah said "yes." In too. He took my hand to come inside when it was tidy

1.2.17 AC see photo
Noah was trying to fill up a watering can at the water butt. He was able to turn the tap by himself and placed his watering can underneath to catch the water. Noah looked to (T) for support to turn the top off. (T) would you give some help Noah? Noah replied yes (T) helped him to turn the top off and showed him which way to push it. Noah lifted his watering can, he looked heavy for him (T) asked Noah if the watering can was "heavy, "yeh" he replied. Noah pored the water out using both hands to control the watering can. Noah then went back to fill his can again and was able to turn the top on and off by himself. Noah was pleased and took his can to pour the water

1.2.17 HM- see photo
Noah initiated conversation with me to show me the bike (T) patting the seat he said "A b..." (T) repeated back "Yes A b..." Noah continued "A b..." He crossed his right leg (furthest away) over the seat and rebalanced as if he was using too-q energy (T) asked Noah if he wanted help to get on. "yes" he responded. (T) directed Noah to use his closest leg to the seat to mount the bike (T) supported Noah to do this. Noah used his feet alternately to push off (T) encouraged Noah to use the pedals. He listened and responded well to the instructor so Noah (T) pushed the bike so Noah could get used to placing his feet on the pedals. Noah fell off and got back on, placing his feet on the pedals independently

1.2.17 HM (No photo)
Noah went on a beam and stretched out each leg behind him in a very controlled manner, as if to gage forward. He then put his arms up as if to gain "foward roll" (T) intervened to explained that he may hurt himself and asked the way and took a clear, safe path to roll and supported Noah to find a clear, safe place to perform the way and took a clear, safe place Noah smiled excitedly if he rolled at Gumtots. Noah found a safe place to perform "...tch" he repeated Noah found a safe place to perform roll independently

Planning in the moment Learning Journey for a child aged 23 months at an outdoor nursery

Learning Journey For ..Ethan........... Date .16 - 6 -.13

Current interests, patterns in learning or information from parents
* cars & trucks
* Enjoys felt pens
* Reading to daisy

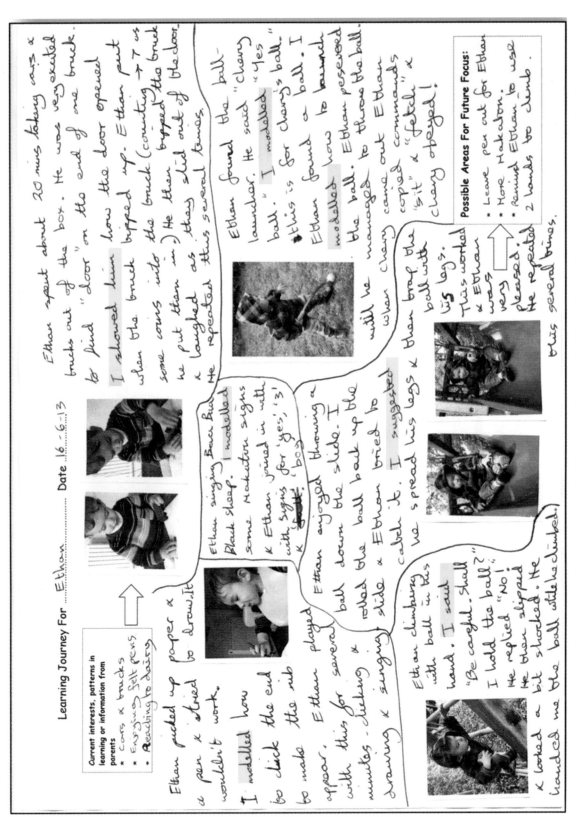

Ethan picked up paper & a pen & tried to draw.It wouldn't work. I modelled how to click the end to make the nib appear. Ethan played with this for several minutes - clicking & singing & drawing & singing.

Ethan singing Baa Baa Black sheep. I modelled some Makaton signs & Ethan joined in with signs for 'yes', '3' with 'box'.

Ethan enjoyed throwing a ball down the slide. I rolled the ball back up the slide & Ethan tried to catch it. I suggested he spread his legs & then trap the ball with his legs.

Ethan climbing with ball in his hand. I said "Be careful. shall I hold the ball?" He replied "No!". He then slipped & then stacked. He handed me the ball still he climbed.

Ethan spent about 20 mins taking cars & trucks out of the box. He was very excited to find "door" on the end of one truck. I showed him how the door opened when the truck tipped up. Ethan put some cars into the truck (counting → 7 as he put them in.) He then tipped the truck & laughed as they slid out of the door. He repeated this several times.

Ethan found the ball - "chang" launcher. He said "yes ball." "I modelled "this is for chang's ball." Ethan found a ball. I modelled how to launch the ball. Ethan persevered to throw the ball until he managed when chang came out Ethan copied commands "sit" & "fetch" & chang obeyed! This worked & Ethan was very pleased. He repeated this several times.

Possible Areas For Future Focus:
* Leave pen out for Ethan
* More Makaton.
* Remind Ethan to use 2 hands to climb.

Planning in the moment Learning Journey for a child aged 26 months with childminder

Learning Journey For Jude .... **Term** Autumn **Week** 5 .... **Date** 31/11/16

C&L	COMMUNICATION AND LANGUAGE	✓
P	PHYSICAL DEVELOPMENT	✓
P	PERSONAL, SOCIAL AND EMOTIONAL DEVELOPMENT	
E	LITERACY	
S	MATHEMATICS	✓
S	UNDERSTANDING THE WORLD	✓
C	EXPRESSIVE ARTS AND DESIGN	✓
	Obs indoors	✓
	Obs outdoors	✓
	Parent consultation	✓

Identified Areas For Focus:
General/Parents:

Profile:
• PSED
• CL
•

Jude was walking peculiarly. The adult modelled the word & sign for toilet. Jude was very wet & needed changing.

Jude approached the adult with the self registration. The adult modelled the children's name & suggested to put them back. Jude said "back"

Jude was playing with the cars. Adult modelled "ready steady go" Jude copied rolling the car on the floor.

A modelled how to use the structure dispenser. Jude then copied.

Jude watched the adult open & close the door under the sand tray. Jude attempted to do it. Adult modelled how to twist the plate to open & close the door. Jude copied. Adult modelled open & close with makaton signs

Jude was playing in the role play area. Adult modelled correct vocabulary for food as Jude preceled it. Jude then said spontaneously "cup of tea", "egg" & "biscuit"

Jude was trying to tear off the cello tape from the dispenser. Adult modelled how to cut it off correctly. Demonstrated four times before

Jude had a go on his own. Jude stuck all the pieces on the paper. Once he got hang of it he was using it correctly over and over again while babbling away

Playing with the lost puzzle. A modelled how to use the finger space to open the door. Jude copied.

Jude was looking at the animal book. He pointed a to the front of the book saying "rabbit, cat, pig, dog & duck" Adult modelled the words butterfly, ladybird, tiger, lion, hamster, starfish & bird with makaton sign. Jude repeated "starfish" & "bird"

Jude is using the hammer on its side so adult modelled the correct way to use the hammer.

Jude was playing with two phones. Jude held one to the adults ear & adult modelled a conversation. Jude copied "baby" & said "1, 2" looking at props.

Jude & some other children had built a ramp. Jude started to climb up. The adult modelled "up, up, up" & then "down, down, down" Later Jude said "P, up, up" & "dan, dan, dan" as he continued his engagement with this activity

Identified Areas For Future Focus:
General/Parents:
Discussed ways of Development.
Profile: promoting speech,
• language & communication
• at home.

Jude was playing in the playhouse. Adult modelled "ball" Jude laughed. Adult continued saying "Wheels" Jude "Jude said "I'm here" Jude continued this with another child

Planning in the moment Learning Journey for child aged 36 months (this child has additional needs) and is in a pack-away pre-school (teaching hi-lighted in green)

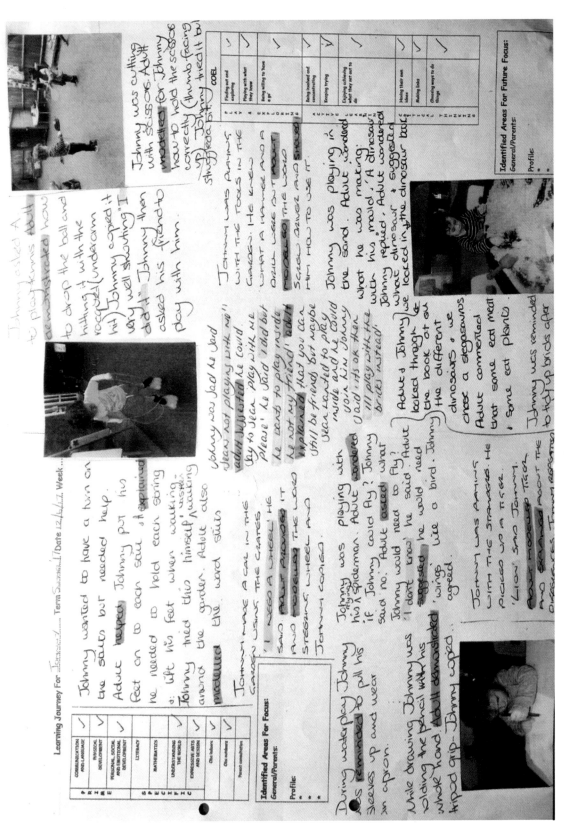

Learning Journey For Johnny..... Term Summer 1/Date 12/6/17. Week...

COMMUNICATION AND LANGUAGE ✓
PHYSICAL DEVELOPMENT ✓
PERSONAL SOCIAL AND EMOTIONAL DEVELOPMENT ✓
LITERACY
MATHEMATICS ✓
UNDERSTANDING THE WORLD
EXPRESSIVE ARTS AND DESIGN ✓

Johnny wanted to have a turn on the slide but needed help. Adult helped Johnny put his feet on to each said & explained he needed to hold each string & lift his feet when wanting to lift himself. Johnny then tried this himself walking around the garden. Adult also modelled the word slide.

Johnny made a cat in the garden using the crates. "I need a wheel" he said. Adult provided it and modelled the word steering wheel and Johnny copied.

During water play Johnny was reminded to pull his sleeves up and wear an apron.

While drawing Johnny was holding the pencil with his whole hand Adult demonstrated tripod grip. Johnny copied.

Johnny was playing with his Spiderman. Adult wondered if Johnny could fly? Johnny said no. Adult asked what Johnny would need to fly? "I don't know" he said. Adult suggested he would need 'wings' like a bird. Johnny agreed.

Johnny was playing with the storages He picked up a tree. 'Lion' said Johnny. Adult modelled tiger and explained about the different stripes Johnny repeated.

Johnny asked A to play. Johnny was not playing with me" Adult suggested he could try to Seca play with me. Please' he said I did but he tends to play inside he is not my friend" Adult explained that you can still be friends but maybe Seca wanted to play inside and he could you join Johnny said it's ok then "I'll play with the bricks instead"

Johnny was playing with the tools in the garden. He knew what a hammer and a drill were but wasn't modelled so the word and showed him how to use it.

Johnny was playing in the sand. Adult wondered what he was making. 'A dinosaur' Johnny replied. Adult wondered what dinosaur & suggested we looked in the dinosaur book

Identified Areas For Focus:
General/Parents:
Profile:

Johnny asked A to play Johnny Adult demonstrated how to drop the ball and hitting it with the racquet (underarm hit) Johnny copied it very well shouting "I did it" Johnny then asked his friend to play with him.

Johnny was cutting with scissors. Adult modelled for Johnny how to hold the scissors correctly (thumb facing up) Johnny tried it by struggled a bit.

COEL
Finding out and exploring ✓
Playing with what they know ✓
Being willing to have a go ✓
Being involved and concentrating ✓
Keeping trying ✓
Enjoying achieving what they set out to do ✓
Having their own ideas ✓
Making links ✓
Choosing ways to do things ✓

Adult & Johnny looked through the book at our the different dinosaurs & we chose a segasaurus. Adult commented that some eat meat & some eat plants.

Johnny was reminded to tidy up bricks after

Identified Areas For Future Focus:
General/Parents:
Profile:

Planning in the moment Learning Journey for a child aged 36 months in a pack-away pre-school (this pre-school uses green hi-lighter for the teaching and yellow for the child's voice)

Learning Journey For **Shareen**...... Term **Spring** Date **14.03.16**

Entries should include the initial observation (& assessment), the teaching and the outcome.

		✓
P	COMMUNICATION AND LANGUAGE	✓
D	PHYSICAL DEVELOPMENT	✓
M	PERSONAL, SOCIAL AND EMOTIONAL DEVELOPMENT	✓
E		
S	LITERACY	✓
P	MATHEMATICS	✓
E	UNDERSTANDING THE WORLD	✓
C		
F	EXPRESSIVE ARTS AND DESIGN	✓
I		
C		
	Obs indoors	✓
	Obs outdoors	✓
	Parent consultation	

Identified Areas For Focus:

General/Parents:
Mum wants to know if we are teaching letter and numbers at nursery.

Profile:
* Building relationships - welcoming
* friends into her games
* Counting with 1:1 correspondence...

Shareen has drawn a picture. Ⓣwonders about the picture - Shareen talks ★ Ⓣ scribes as she talks. Ⓣ suggests Shareen could do some writing. Shareen writes on the page - left to right, Ⓣ moving down the page.

Shareen looking at biscuit book Ⓣ encouraged her to count spoons. Shareen said "two." Ⓣ modelled counting from "one," Shareen counting 1-4 with 1:1 correspondence. Carterhatch

"I going to do fix it" Shareen holds nail, fingers at the top and hammers 'ouch! I hurt finger.' Ⓟ Support Shareen to hold nail correctly. Shareen hammers nail into wood confidently 'ooce, I do this many.' Ⓣ wonder 'too many'. Shareen counts 'nails' 1, 2, 4' Ⓣ suggest Shareen follow Ⓣ explains 'I want pizza.' Ⓣ suggest He 'Six' and another one Ⓣ monitor 'more 2' Ⓣ Shareen 1, 2, 3, 4, 5, 6.

Shareen appears to enjoy making Pizza. "What they cooking." Ⓣ explains 'I want pizza.' Ⓣ suggest making pizza herself. Ⓣ explain Ⓣ 'ingredient' Ⓣ onion, cheese Ⓣ model cutting onions Shareen cuts returns to work nails safely ★ independently

up onion adding ingredient on to her pizza.
Shareen cook Shareen cut a grows with her friends

Shareen got off the bike a left it in middle of garden. Ⓣ reminds her to put it away. Ⓣ encouraged her to count the number on the bike. Shareen joined Ⓣ counting 1-8. Shareen looked & found correct space for the bike.

Shareen mark making Ⓣ wonder "I'm wonder high" Shareen works. eyes, nose, mouth. Ⓣ wonder 'what else.' 'arm, hand' Ⓣ suggest toe. Ⓣ face. 'eyes' 'nose' Ⓣ point 'eyebrows.' Shareen mark her face including details Ⓣwith correct Ⓣ pen grip.

Shareen found her friend looking under logs for insects. 'It look like a sweets.' Shareen finds slug. Ⓣ comment on bright colour and detail on body. Shareen uses a magnifying glass to look closer. Ⓣ demonstrates how to hold it close to slug. She watches it closely telling friends and staff 'look I've found 4 slugs.'

Shareen smells the garlic bulbs 'um nice.' Ⓣ wonder if you use garlic at home in your cooking? Children talk about 'daag, nie, pak' Ⓣ encourages her plant bulbs and demonstrate using tools Ⓣ helps and breaks Shareen repeats instruction down, dig, and use tools effectively to dig hole, to plant and water to bulb. Ⓣ praises.

I want Zip the fleece Ⓣ demonstrates how you do it to me.' Ⓣ support Shareen by Shareen follow Ⓣ instruction and zips her coat 'it's hard' Ⓣ praises.

Identified Areas For Future Focus:

General/Parents:
Mum to read a story everyday with Shareen.

Profile:
- To count at home -
  - walking up steps.
  - as she puts her dinner away - how many meatballs now?
- getting dressed in the morning - counting items of clothing in...

Learning Journey For ...TND..... Term Autumn Date 5/10/15

Entries should include the initial observation (& assessment), the teaching and the outcome. ←see photo in ⑨

P	COMMUNICATION AND LANGUAGE			✓
R	PHYSICAL DEVELOPMENT			✓
I.	PERSONAL, SOCIAL AND EMOTIONAL			✓
W	DEVELOPMENT			
E	LITERACY			✓
S	MATHEMATICS			✓
P	UNDERSTANDING THE WORLD			✓
E				
C				
T	EXPRESSIVE ARTS AND DESIGN			✓
F				
H	Obs indoors			✓
I	Obs outdoors			✓
C	consultation			

Identified Areas For Focus:

General/Parents:
Speaking?

Profile:
* Setting into reception
* Enjoying a wide range
* of activities

Two draws a spider red & silver on sequins he shows T. Loud T praises/wonders spider. T asks Two to write his name. Two uses namecard. Two indicates his face to facepaint. T paints Two face & shares pic of carpet time with class.

Two shows T this woodwork. T wonders Is horse. T praises. Two wonders about eyes & how T provides some paint. Yes T provides some paint. Two chooses length & cuts he nails to read & adds eyes. T provides Pad to search hobby horses Two spots ears and wheels. Two adds ears then shows T this mouth. Two makes cutting wood with saw to show line. My mouth. Two adds to horse using same technique. T provides wheels. Two hammers first one on too. Two hammers by hammering tight he adjusts by hammering nail out a bit then checks wheel can turn he repeats with second wheel. T like praises praises.

Two is looking at books in reading area ties to little monkeys jumping on the bed. very loud. T praises/reminds inside voice

Two watches Layla-Rae make a puppet show 2 puppets. T asks Two if he would like to help. Yes he selects lolly stick and sticks on material, a animal. he says

which animal, a tiger.

Two makes wooden ears. he wants wood up to puppet he laughs. T's eyes and too big. he goes back to wood work bench & makes them smaller. ⊙ supports him when cutting out puppet theatre

Two made a puppet show. + wanted to write a story for it. Two write his name independently ① introduced letter caf. + showed T the letters he needed. Two wrote these some letter formation. ② showed T the number line. ③ suggested counting along the line looking for the numbers he needed. T shared his story with the class. see 3 & 16

Two works with Archie in tree house pulling up bucket & pulling up. ⊙ models pull it up. & help me Archie. Two repeats ① introduces them to pulleys in sand area. The boys continue to work together.

General/Parents: At home model language - if Two speaks English.

Profile:
* Building confidence with speaking
* speaking by modelling language when he uses one word.

Areas For Future Focus:

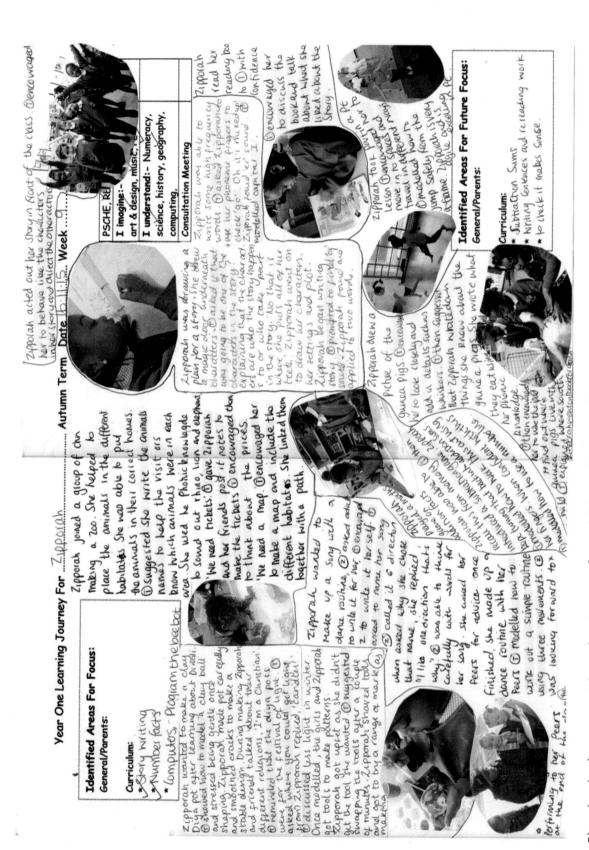

Year One Learning Journey For ....Zipporah....   Autumn Term Date 16.11.15 Week 9

Identified Areas For Focus:

General/Parents:

Curriculum:
* Story Writing
* Number facts
* Computers - Program the beebot

I imagine:- art & design, music,

I understand:- Numeracy, science, history, geography, computing.

Consultation Meeting

PSCHE, RE

Planning in the moment Learning Journey for a child aged 70 months in a Year One class

Identified Areas For Future Focus:

General/Parents:

Curriculum:
* Subtraction Sums
* Writing sentences and re-reading work
* to check it makes sense.

DATE. 10 - 14th July ...TERM... Summer ....WEEK..........................

FOCUS CHILDREN: * O.O , P.B   * I.S   *

· composed sector J
  Otto .J.

	PRIME AREAS			SPECIFIC AREAS			
AREAS COVERED	C&L	PHD	PSE	LIT	MATHS	UW	EA&D
	✓	✓	✓	✓	✓✓	✓	✓

MONDAY	am TUESDAY pm	am WEDNESDAY pm	am THURSDAY pm	am FRIDAY pm
am pm	⑤ ⑥			
① ③ ② ④	⑦			

Outcome

	Observation	Outcome/Activity	Next Steps/Completed
1	Children not using sand timers appropriately Photo (HM)	(T) explained what they are for, suggesting chn see what 3 mins feels by doing 3 mins yoga. (T) read "What's the time Mr. Wolf" drawing attention to time vocabulary	Chn shared their ideas in a discussion about time, making their own links to the clock
2	Children in mud pie kitchen making 'cakes'.	(T) provided paper cake cases to enhance play. Encouraged children to think about what flavour their cakes were and how they were making them. Encouraged imaginative role play of a 'café' by ordering food.	Chn continued to make cakes. Took on roles of 'chef' and 'waitress' and engaged in role play taking orders from each other and staff. see photo
3	Children using the wooden blocks to build towers, unable to reach the top to make it taller.	(T) showed how they could make a step with the blocks to reach the top. Modelled language of taller, smaller etc when encouraging children to think about whether their tower was taller or shorter than them.	Chn continued building towers and enjoyed using their hands (marking across from their head) to see if their tower was taller than them. see photos.
4	Child used a straw to directly blow into paint pot causing it to flick up at his face.	(T) explained that you can use straws to blow paint but you don't put the straw directly in it. (T) demonstrated to interested group	Chn continued to explore patterns made when blowing paint safely see photo's
5	chn letting cars down the ramps and tunes	(T) provided paint and paper adding them to the ramp (T) suggested printing the car wheels and letting them go	chn dipped cars and drove into paint making marks as they rolled down the paper. chn observed colours mixing no photo
6	chn trying to make sandcastles and becoming frustrated that they kept breaking when they tipped their buckets over	(T) wondered what might help make their sandcastles work, chn knew what would help as the sand needed to be wet. (T) provided water in the sand pit	chn were able to make sandcastles. no photo

PHOTO GALLERY ON REVERSE

Planning in the moment Group sheet from an outdoor nursery.

(The headings on this sheet have now been changed to "Observation", "Teaching", "Outcome".)

W/C: 12·5·14   **Term:** Summer   **Week:** 4   **Page:** 2   Carterhatch

Focus Children:

*   *   *   *

*   *   *   *

	PRIME AREAS			SPECIFIC AREAS			
	C&L	PHD	PSE	LIT	MATHS	UW	EXP A&D
	✓	✓	✓	✓	✓	✓	✓

Monday	Tuesday	Wednesday	Thursday	Friday

	Observation and Assessment	(Plan and) Teaching	Outcome (Observation)
1:	Chn finding snails. and putting them in water.	ⓣ Spoke to chn about snails not being able to swim ⓣ suggested they make the snails a house and find them food to eat,	Made snails houses on woodwork bench
2:	Chn looking at Beans growing up walks.	Chn guessing how far they would grow in 1 day. ⓣ provided sticker for them to mark poles to monitor growth.	
3:	Chn interested in making witches hats + wands.	ⓣ modelled how to make the hats & chn decide to stick them together with sticky tape. ⓣ provided resources for wands + models how to make	that. chn then decide on the magic words they will use.
4:	Chn wanted to know where snails mouth was.	ⓣ Put snail on door so they could see underneath it	Children observed how snail moved + mouth parts
5:	Chn running around screaming	ⓣ Suggested they play 'What the time Mr Wolf' - chn Counting out, taking turns to be Crof.	
6:	Chn complaining that it was hot.	ⓣ spoke to chn about ways to cool down. They decided to they wanted a paddling pool.	- Took off own shoes and put them on. - followed ⓣ instruction - no jumping/runn in the water.

Photo's

Planning in the moment Group sheet from a school nursery class

Spontaneous Planning

w/c 31/10/16 Term: Aut 2

Focus Children:
· Navraj · Jenson · Amaka

Areas Covered	Prime Areas			Specific Areas			
	C&L	PHD	PSED	LIT	MATHS	UW	EAD
	✓	✓	✓	✓	✓	✓	✓

Monday	Tuesday	Wednesday	Thursday	Friday
✓	✓	✓		—

	Observation and Assessment	(Plan and) Teaching	Outcome (observation)
1	Chn were looking at bugs in the mud kitchen, they had found a lady bird.	I encouraged chn to use the investigation area and equipment - I modelled how to use the equipment. I suggested lots of different areas where we could look for bugs - I explained the differences between the bugs we found and wondered if the chn knew anything	Chn could use investigation equipment. Chn could describe what they saw and find new areas around the playgr to find the bugs/insects
2	Chn heard the tractor outside	I wondered if they would like to see it. I explained how to stay safe by sitting on the wall, I encouraged chn to look closely at what the tractor was doing	Chn were able to sit safely on the wall, some were able to notice features such as the grass getting sho
3	Chn wanted to play basketball	I provided a cone lane + a net, I explain the rules of the game, I modelled patting the ball to move it. I encouraged chn to have a try. I suggested lining up to take turns	chn found controlling the ball tricky, all chn were able to take turns
4	Chn noticed Rangoli patterns and asked about them	I explained about Diwali. I provided a video showing how Diwali is celebrated, I encouraged chn to share their experiences	some chn were able to talk about their own Diwali experiences
5	Chn made a train using Poddely.	I suggested chn work together to make their model. I explained we needed a tick to ride a train, I encouraged chn to write tickets and say where they were going	Chn were able to work together and all could make marks and say what it meant
6	Chn wanted to play with bubbles.	I suggested chn use bubbles by turn taking. I encouraged them to get a pen + whiteboard and estimate how many bubbles we might blow chn wrote down the numbers they thought. I encouraged chn to take turns blowing the bubbles	chn were able to write an estimation with support. chn coul take t blow bubbles independently
7	Chn wanted to paint	I provided water colour paints, I explained they needed water to work. I modelled painting with the paints I encouraged chn to have a try	Chn were able to use the paints to make colour wash pictures and some noticed changin colours

Photo Gallery

Planning in the moment Group sheet from a Reception class – Autumn Term

pontaneous Planning

Wc 27/3   Term Sp2

cus Children:

Conor · Ruby · Lawand.

Areas Covered	Prime Areas			Specific Areas			
	C&L	PHD	PSED	LIT	MATHS	UW	EAD
	✓	✓	✓	✓	✓	✓	✓

Monday	Tuesday	Wednesday	Thursday	Friday
✓	✓	✓	✓	✓

	Observation and Assessment	(Plan and) Teaching	Outcome (observation)
1	Chn were playing with the hairdressing box and pretending to be hairdressers	I encouraged chn to help set up a hairdressers, using the mirrors, chairs, setting out the hair equipment. I modelled how to use the hair tools and suggested they try using them with their hands, and encouraged them to take turns, sharing the equipment ... you could also ask questions to one another "How would you like... what colour" etc	Chn could help set up. They could share, take turns and use the equipment for one game & able to use questions to one another, asking what they did and didn't like - more creative 5
2	Chn were running around the playground	I suggested we play duck, duck goose. I explained how to play I modelled running around the circle and finding a space I encouraged chn to choose chn that want had a turn	Chn were able to enjoy their running in the circle. They were able to take turns fairly
3	Chn wanted to be police officers	I provided role play equipment I worked what police do I suggested setting up a police station I explained how to write a report form I encouraged chn to share	Chn were able to say what they thought police officers do and shared this in
4	Chn wanted to skip	I encouraged chn to make I line I suggested counting skips in 10's I modelled counting each movement in 10's	Chn were able to count accurately in 10's > 100
5	Chn continued police role play	I suggested chn build a police station I explained police officers have note books to write about 'bad guys' I provided note books + pencils. I encouraged chn to use books	Chn were able to use phonic knowledge to sound out some words for writing
6	Chn were making a "volcano"	I wondered how they had made it. I asked if we needed anything else, I suggested chn share ideas	Chn were able to share ideas about finishing the volcano and worked together to a...
7	Chn wanted to make a obstacle course	I suggested chn help make an obstacle course. I wondered if they could find appropriate objects to use to make this. I demonstrated how to put these together. I encouraged chn to add more to make our obstacle trickier and more challenging	Chn could help eachother build. Chn could find appro... objects that were s... for climbing on and design an obstacle c... that involved having to climb

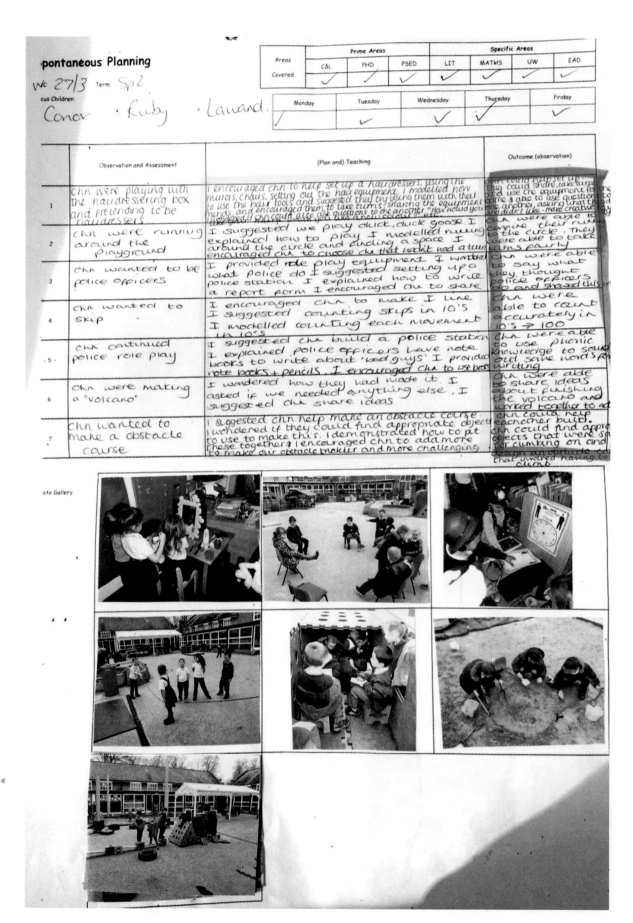

oto Gallery

Planning in the moment Group sheet from a Reception class – Spring Term

6 Assessment and record-keeping

Assessments and evidence – practitioner's knowledge

Most assessments, and the evidence, about children are in the practitioner's head. If an attentive parent is asked about their child, they would be able to tell you about them in detail. They would know exactly what the child is interested in, what makes them anxious, what makes them laugh, whether the child can tolerate practical jokes, what frightens them, whether they can draw a circle, how they like to be comforted, what they eat, whether they can use scissors, their medical history, how confident they are in different situations, whether they speak two languages, and so on – the list could go on for ever. Such a parent is able to make assessments accurately and confidently. However, none of this is documented – so how does the parent know all this? They know because they have spent time with their child – watching them, listening to them, playing with them, talking with them in numerous situations, and doing a variety of activities. If you have your own children, you know that this is the case. You do not need to go and look in a book to find out if your child can walk up the stairs confidently – you have seen them do it hundreds of times. **It is the same for attentive practitioners in a setting. They know the children in great detail and can make assessments confidently and accurately without referring to bits of paper or other forms of evidence**.

However, in many settings, practitioners spend hours each week writing up notes, printing and annotating photographs, cross-referencing observations to statements in Development Matters, gathering pictures that a child has drawn, and so on. This practice is hugely time-consuming, whether contributing to paper records (often known as special books) or electronic systems (which are becoming more popular). When I ask practitioners why they are keeping such vast amounts of evidence about each child, there are various responses: "Because my manager says that we have to do this", "Ofsted will demand to see the evidence to back up our assessments" or "The parents really like it". My question would be: "If the documentation and evidence bank that you are producing does not directly support the development of the children, then why are you producing it?" As stated earlier, practitioners spend so much time producing elaborate folders of evidence to "*prove*" progress, that they reduce the amount of time spent interacting with (i.e. teaching) the children and, therefore, progress is reduced.

Practitioners need to regain their confidence and say: **"I know these children. I can make accurate assessments based on my knowledge. I am a professional and I should be trusted. I should not have to prove my knowledge by producing meaningless banks of evidence."** The EYFS Handbook has a useful quote regarding evidence that practitioners should collect:

> Evidence doesn't need to be formally recorded or documented. The extent to which the practitioner chooses to record information will depend on individual preference. Paperwork should be kept to the minimum that practitioners need to illustrate, support and recall their knowledge of the child's attainment
> 2017 Early Years Foundation Stage:
> Assessment and Reporting Arrangements

Ofsted have also produced a myth-busting document which states: "Fact: There is no prescribed way of conducting or recording assessments, as long as it is effective and helps children's learning, development and progress" (Guidance Early Years Inspections: Myths – updated 3 April, 2017).

When practitioners spend the vast majority of their time *going to the children, observing them and interacting with them,* they are assessing constantly, even if many are unaware of this. They are noticing things all the time and this information is retained, whether consciously or not. This formative assessment not only helps them decide how to respond in that moment but also contributes to their bank of knowledge about the particular child. This knowledge is then drawn upon when it comes to the time to complete a summative assessment (often involving entering assessments into an electronic tracking system) perhaps as an "on entry" assessment or at the end of a term. These practitioners can complete such summative assessments with ease. Just as the attentive parent can complete such assessments for their own child, an attentive practitioner can do the same for the children in their setting.

At the time of writing this book, the vast majority of settings in England are using the age bands and statements within Development Matters as a reference point for their assessments. It should be noted that there is no legal requirement to use this, or any other, specific document. At this time, practitioners are legally required to carry out a check on children at two years of age (often referred to as the "two year check") and to assess whether children have achieved the early learning goals at the end of Reception. There are proposals to make changes to these legal requirements but, as this book goes to print, there have been no final decisions about changes. At this time, therefore, practitioners can decide what reference point they use for their assessments and tracking. They could opt, for example, to use the tracker that has been produced by Early Excellence. Their tracker does not involve best-fit judgements; rather it has "key indicator" statements relating to a child's chronological age and also includes some "weighting" relating to the characteristics of effective learning. Individual settings can decide how they are going to track children and what evidence to collect. Whatever changes are introduced by the government, practitioners must remain confident that their own complex and detailed knowledge of children cannot be represented or replaced by any amount of paper evidence, electronic records or a test.

While there is no requirement to keep documented evidence, it is advisable to have a systematic way of gathering some documentation for each child. The systems described in Chapter 5 give practitioners enough evidence to satisfy any external body, but they also mean that children have a unique, personal record of their time in a setting. Equally, parents have examples that track and demonstrate their child's experiences and development during their time in a setting.

When practitioners input their summative assessments to a tracker (be that electronic or paper-based), they will begin to see if there are any "gaps". For example, if they are struggling to make assessments of a certain aspect of development they should consider whether their environment needs adapting in order to offer children opportunities that will cover this. For example, in one school, the staff were used to delivering music lessons and found that, without these, they were less confident in assessing this aspect of the children's development. They decided that this was because the children did not have access to instruments and music on a regular basis. As soon as some instruments and a CD player were introduced to the outdoor area, this "gap" immediately disappeared and the staff became completely confident in their assessments of this aspect of learning.

I am often told about **inspectors who ask to see things which they are not supposed to ask to see**. Examples of this include literacy books in Reception, whole class teaching sessions, written evidence for each area of development, plans for focussed tasks, a chance to watch an adult-led session, tracking based on Development Matters, documentation relating to "next steps" and so on. **None of these should be requested and none of these are a legal requirement**. Practitioners need to know their legal requirements and what inspectors are permitted to request. They must then be confident in challenging such requests.

An HMI (Her Majesty's Inspectorate) gave me some good advice on this point. She said that if an inspector requests to see something that they are not supposed to ask for, then the practitioner should say: **"I am really sorry, I am really confused. Please could you show me in your handbook where it says that I need to do that."** The inspector will then need to apologise and withdraw the request.

Together we need to take back ownership of our profession and operate from a position of confidence in our pedagogy, rather than from a position of fear and top-down pressure. Let us keep the paperwork minimised and our knowledge maximised, because this is what will most benefit the children.

> *This all just made sense to me. When my own children were little, I didn't plan what they were going to make or do. I started to question why I was trying to control everything that the children in my care were doing. I had lost my nerve. I kept worrying that they wouldn't make progress if I didn't make them do all these planned activities. But once I let go, I was amazed. The children were so relaxed, so busy, so happy . . . and so was I. No going back now. I have got my weekends back. No more wasted hours planning activities that no child is interested in . . . and they are still making great progress!*

Childminder, Blackpool, **2017**

Our outside area is very well used and has seen the inclusion of a work bench, trapeze and climbing frame, all ensuring children regularly take risks and challenge themselves, learning to become confident in their own abilities and their capacity to learn through practice and persistence.

To sum up, the change has given us the freedom to teach in accordance with children's needs and in a way that is nourishing for them and us.

Chris Dingley, Gunter Primary School, Birmingham, **2017**

Planning in the moment has transformed both our practice and ourselves here at Gunter. It has taken us from interferers to interacters, privileged to play with the children in our setting. The differences before ITMP (In the Moment Planning) and since, are measurable; in the environment, the way it is organised and what is included and also in the behaviours of children and staff. Gone is the "teacher voice" raised above that of the children, leading to a setting that is calmer and more harmonious, which is widely commented on by parents and visitors alike. For me, I am teaching/playing at my highest level and enjoying every moment in the classroom, developing close relationships with the children, knowing their interests, strengths and ways in which to support them, in a way I only hoped for before. I have become a mother to a setting full of children, sharing in their awe, wonder and spontaneity. Each day is a new and exciting journey embarked on with both children and staff alike, working/playing at the highest levels of involvement. Most significantly for the children is the change in their Characteristics of Effective Learning. Children are demonstrating far higher levels of interest and involvement, persevering and showing a "can do" attitude whilst creativity and critical thinking is all over the shop and motivation for all is evident in the constant thrum of activity.

Staff are animated and so knowledgeable about the children and free to focus on what's next, (rather than spending time planning ahead), becoming experts in planning in the now and interacting to extend and deepen the children's learning, whilst continually reflecting on the EYFS curriculum. For the teaching staff, planning, preparation and assessment is now a celebration of children's learning. Inputting the children's "Wow!" moments, contributed by all the staff, is a delight and leads naturally to knowing what's next. Time is freed up to reconsider the environment and provision, to visit the KEYU Facebook page, and similar, in order to take on further inspiration and to continue tweaking and enhancing. We now have more time to look at our setting through the eyes of visitors and our children and to share and seek out good practice and continue to be reflective.

Our environment which offered good continuous provision before the implementation of ITMP is experiencing its latest transformation into one that includes natural materials and storage. This is directly impacting children's creativity as they use resources in ways that we could not imagine. Interestingly, as we were half way through this process, children showed a preference for the materials in the natural baskets as opposed to the plastic. Staff and children feel calmer as the setting is becoming more homely and less traditionally "school" like.

Chris Dingley, Gunter Primary School, Birmingham, **2017**

What helps most in the long run is the ability to enter into the child's own world with an informed sympathy, the general sense that his problems are problems of growth, and a patient and friendly interest in the ways of that growth.

Susan Isaacs, *The Nursery Years*, Routledge & Kegan Paul, London, **1929**

ACTION PLAN

Trial a focus child sheet and discuss as a staff. Check that entries include "observation, teaching, outcome".

Discuss how well you feel you know the focus child at the end of the week. Would you be confident to make assessments about this child?

Trial a Group sheet (if you work with children over the age of three years old).

Discuss how the activities that emerge differ from activities that you have pre-planned in the past.

Conclusion

I am opening this conclusion with the same words as those used in the Introduction – **planning in the moment is nothing new**. It is exactly what a responsive parent does with their child every day. It is exactly what skilful practitioners have always done. Every time an adult looks at, and listens to, a child, they are assessing and "planning" how to respond. These assessments and plans are based on the adult's observations of the child in that moment and also draw on any previous knowledge of the child. The response is "planned" **in the moment** and is uniquely suited to that unique child in that unique moment. The adult will be considering (either consciously or instinctively) whether they can add anything in that moment to benefit the child. If so, they will respond and interact accordingly, supporting the child to develop.

The initial idea of this book was to give practitioners a quick guide to "planning in the moment". However, once I started to write the book it became clear that this would not be possible. I have worked with thousands of children over a period of more than 40 years. What this has taught me is that in **the best practice, the children are initiating their own play**, the practitioners are joining the children and they are then planning in the moment, deciding if, and how, to respond. This means that in the best settings, the children are initiating the play and not the adults. The adults in this situation remain observant,

interested and responsive – ready to interact if they feel they can add anything to the play. This book, therefore, needed to give a rationale as to why child-initiated play is so powerful and then explore how this could be organised.

In brief, this book gives the following messages:

- When children are displaying deep levels of involvement there is increased brain activity and synapse formation (i.e. learning).
- Deep-level involvement is seen when children have autonomy and genuine choice (which is what they have during child-initiated play).
- Deep-level involvement indicates maximum learning and low-level involvement indicates minimal learning.
- Therefore, give the children autonomy and choice and allow them to initiate their own play for the maximum amount of time possible.
- Remove all activities and routines that result in low-level involvement as they are a waste of everyone's time and energy.

This then leads to the conclusion that the most important feature of any early years setting is child-initiated play – that is, allowing children to select what to do. They will select what engages them, what interests them and what challenges them, because it is innate in a child to want to learn – to want to be deeply involved. For some, the image of "play" might then need to shift. "Play" should be viewed as anything that delivers deep involvement for a particular child. As each child is unique, so too is their play. Every child wants to be deeply involved and each will achieve this in their own unique way. The hugely complex task for practitioners is to ensure that this is possible and to clarify the role of the adult within this play.

At this point, it becomes critical to consider the emotional well-being of the children because, although all children want to be deeply involved, this is not possible if their well-being is not high. For children in a setting, the relationships, transition, induction, consistencies, boundaries, routines, activities and so on, can all have an effect on well-being. Therefore, all these aspects of practice are explored within this book. In addition, but beyond the scope of this book, are all the external influences on young children which can so dramatically impact on their ability to feel secure at any time.

Once children feel secure, then the environment and the role of the adults within a setting, determine whether deep levels of involvement will be achieved. Therefore, the book explores these aspects of child-initiated play – how to create an enabling environment and the role of the adult within that environment.

The paperwork that we have developed over the last ten years is explained in Chapter 5 but this chapter cannot be read in isolation. The chapter explains how the paperwork is a record of a tiny proportion of the learning and teaching that takes place within any setting. However, it is the "play" itself that is critical to success. In a setting, if the majority of children are displaying deep levels of involvement for the majority of the time, then we know that deep-level learning is happening. The paperwork then becomes far less important – it is a distraction from the play. However, the systems described in Chapter 5

have been tried and tested and they do deliver a good balance between providing some documentation of learning, while allowing practitioners to spend the vast majority of their time interacting with (i.e. teaching) the children as they play.

This book has taken far longer to write than expected. This is partly due to the complexities of the pedagogy, as explained above. However, it is also because of my total fascination with my granddaughter, who was born as I started to write this book and who is seven months old as I write this conclusion. She is now able to move around in her own unique way. She communicates by blowing bubbles when she is annoyed, squealing when something is funny, raising her arms to be picked up and also responding to a few Makaton signs. She now notices when her mum moves away and she is not always willing to accept this. Her innate desire to learn could not be more evident. She demands to be "engaged" – i.e. she is content when there is something, or often someone, that interests her and with which she can become deeply involved. Luckily, she has adults around her who are responsive, who "plan in the moment" according to their observations. Therefore, she can remain deeply involved for as much of her waking hours as possible. She will eventually go to a nursery and her innate desire to learn will still be there. But she is unique and, like all children, she needs a setting that will value that uniqueness and support it to flourish. She will need adults who are fascinated by her, willing to observe her and respond to her – i.e. **she will need adults who are planning in the moment**. She will need an environment that is "enabling" in the broadest sense. She needs the freedom to learn in the best possible way – through her play!

I urge practitioners to reflect on their practice in terms of how well it supports the deepest levels of involvement for the children. Trust that this is a powerful measure of success. Understand why and how this can be achieved through **child-initiated play and planning in the moment**. Each practitioner can then plan how to move along their journey to make this successful for their setting – whatever that setting may be. Every child deserves this opportunity and it is the responsibility of practitioners to provide it. By reading this book carefully, practitioners can explore this journey – from the rationale that explains the value of child-initiated play, through the complex practicalities of environments and interactions and, finally, to some ideas about the paperwork that is needed in order to support this. The journey will vary depending on your starting point.

> It took a year to begin a trial in my school nursery. In May 2016, I read Nursery Year in Action and then lent it to the Early Years' lead and the nursery team. In November "in the moment planning" was mentioned positively on a headteachers' course. Our local authority booked Anna Ephgrave for a conference and my TA and I came back buzzing. In March, I found a local school using "in the moment planning" and arranged for the whole Foundation Stage team, the Early Years' lead and the headteacher to visit. In April, we got the go ahead for a trial. First, we replaced adult-led focused activities during child-initiated play with "in the moment planning" recording on the Group sheet. In May, we swapped our long observations (and next step follow-up intervention system) for the focus child system. In July 2017, I briefed new parents in a meeting about how it works and cautioned them not to expect Christmas, Easter cards, etc. Little steps, seed planting and patience (which is the hardest bit when you're excited) paid off.

Rachel Dickens, Nursery teacher, Henry Bradley Infant School, Chesterfield, **2017**

I stress again – children want to learn. However, they each want to learn in their own unique way. The organisation of a setting that makes this possible is extremely complex. **Forward planning of activities or learning objectives does not support this uniqueness, nor does it maximise progress.**

Each child can flourish, and progress can be maximised, if the practitioners:

- develop a meaningful relationship with each child and their family;
- provide a superb enabling environment;
- establish clear and consistent boundaries and expectations;
- give children **long periods** of child-initiated play (with genuine autonomy and choice);
- remain observant and fascinated and;
- **plan in the moment** – teaching next steps **in the moment too!**

To conclude, reflect on your practice in terms of how well it supports the deepest levels of involvement for the children. Trust that this is a powerful, objective, measure of success. Read this book to help you understand why, and how, the deepest involvement is achieved through **child-initiated play** supported by **planning in the moment**.

Finally, it is a wise general rule to leave the children free to use their playthings in their own way – even if this does not happen to be the way that we might think the best. For play has the greatest value for the young child when it is really free and his own.

Susan Isaacs, *The Nursery Years*, Routledge & Kegan Paul, London, **1929**

Appendix A: Levels of Involvement

Ferre Laevers

Involvement focuses on the extent to which pupils are operating to their full capabilities. In particular it refers to whether the child is focused, engaged and interested in various activities.

The Leuven Scale for Involvement specifies:

1 Low activity
Activity at this level can be simple, stereotypic, repetitive and passive. The child is absent and displays no energy. There is an absence of cognitive demand. The child characteristically may stare into space. N.B. This may be a sign of inner concentration.

2 A frequently interrupted activity
The child is engaged in an activity but half of the observed period includes moments of non-activity, in which the child is not concentrating and is staring into space. There may be frequent interruptions in the child's concentration, but his/her involvement is not enough to return to the activity.

3 Mainly continuous activity
The child is busy at an activity but it is at a routine level and the real signals for involvement are missing. There is some progress but energy is lacking and concentration is at a routine level. The child can be easily distracted.

4 Continuous activity with intense moments
The child's activity has intense moments during which activities at Level 3 can come to have special meaning. Level 4 is reserved for the kind of activity seen in those intense moments, and can be deduced from the "Involvement signals". This level of activity is resumed after interruptions. Stimuli from the surrounding environment, however attractive, cannot seduce the child away from the activity.

5 Sustained intense activity
The child shows continuous and intense activity revealing the greatest involvement. During the observed period not all the signals for involvement need be there, but the essential ones must be present: concentration, creativity, energy and persistence. This intensity must be present for almost all the observation period.

Level of Involvement

Time	Involvement	Comments
Average		

Appendix B: Playdough recipe

You need:

1 cup salt
2 cups plain flour
4 teaspoons cream of tartar
2 tablespoons cooking oil
2 cups boiling water
Food colouring
Large bowl

Mix all the ingredients in a large bowl.

If the dough is kept in a plastic bag or an airtight container, it will last approximately six weeks.

Appendix C: Biscuit recipe

 **flour**

sugar

butter

Mix, roll and cut the biscuit shapes.
Cook at 150° C for 25 minutes or until golden brown.

Cake Recipe

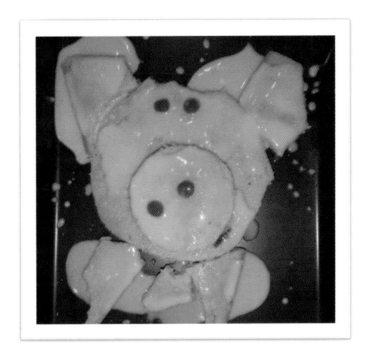

You can use

1 egg or

2 eggs or 3 eggs or

4 eggs or 5 eggs or 6 eggs

More eggs = bigger cake!

Balance the eggs with the flour.

Put the flour in the bowl.

~ 1 ~

Balance the eggs with the sugar.

Put the sugar in the bowl.

~ 2 ~

Balance the eggs with the butter.

Put the butter in the bowl.

~ 3 ~

Add the eggs to the bowl.

Mix, mix, mix!

~ 4 ~

Put the mixture in a baking tray.

Cook at 180° C for 15 minutes.

Decorate your cake and eat it!

~ 5 ~

Appendix E: Focus child letter

Planning for your child's Learning Journey

Next week we will be focusing on _____. We will be observing them while they play to find out more about their interests and how they are progressing. Please take some pictures (**no more than 15**) of your child/family enjoying activities out of school.

We value the knowledge and understanding you have of your child and would really appreciate it if you would share this with us so that we can work together to meet your child's needs.

Is there anything significant happening in your child's life at the moment e.g. visits, holidays, new pets, family celebrations? Is there anything you would like to tell us about your child?

Is there anything you would like to ask us about your child's progress and development?

Please return this sheet with the camera by _____.

Please ensure that the camera is used with adult supervision, kept away from water and no objects are placed on the camera's LED screen.

Thank you.

Appendix F: Learning Journey (children under 36 months)

Learning Journey for .... Date ....

Entries should include the initial observation (and assessment), the teaching and the outcome.

Current interests, patterns in learning or information from parents:

*

*

*

Possible Areas for Future Focus:

*

*

*

Appendix G: Learning Journey for nursery and Reception children

Learning Journey for .... Term .... Date ....

Entries should include the initial observation (and assessment), the teaching and the outcome.	

P R I M E	COMMUNICATION AND LANGUAGE
	PHYSICAL DEVELOPMENT
	PERSONAL, SOCIAL AND EMOTIONAL DEVELOPMENT
S P E C I F I C	LITERACY
	MATHEMATICS
	UNDERSTANDING THE WORLD
	EXPRESSIVE ARTS AND DESIGN
	Obs indoors
	Obs outdoors
	Parent consultation

Identified Areas for Focus:

General/Parents:

Profile:

*

*

*

Identified Areas for Future Focus:

General/Parents:

Profile:

*

*

*

Appendix H: Year One Learning Journey

Year One Learning Journey for .... Date ....

PSCHE, RE	
I imagine: Literacy, D and T, art and design, music, PE	
I understand: Numeracy, science, history, geography, computing	
Consultation Meeting	

Identified Areas for Focus:

General/Parents:

Curriculum:

*

*

*

Identified Areas for Future Focus:

Appendix I: Ofsted definition of teaching

Teaching should not be taken to imply a "top down" or formal way of working. It is a broad term that covers the many different ways in which adults help young children learn. It includes their interactions with children during planned and child-initiated play and activities: communicating and modelling language, showing, explaining, demonstrating, exploring ideas, encouraging, questioning, recalling, providing a narrative for what they are doing, facilitating and setting challenges. It takes account of the equipment adults provide and the attention given to the physical environment, as well as the structure and routines of the day that establish expectations.

Ofsted, September, 2015

Appendix J: Group sheet

PRIME AREAS			SPECIFIC AREAS			
C & L	PHD	PSE	LIT	MATHS	UW	EXP A & D

W/C:.............................. Term:................................

Focus Children:*   *   *

Monday	Tuesday	Wednesday	Thursday	Friday

	Observation & Assessment	(Plan &) Teaching	Outcome (observation)
1			
2			
3			
4			
5			
6			

Photo Gallery:

Appendix K: Suppliers

www.creativecascade.co.uk – for Creative Cascade Sets, welly storage, woodwork benches and Funky Fountains. (Products designed by Anna!)

Skips, ditches, parents (great suppliers of "junk modelling" resources), charity shops, etc.

DIY stores and on-line companies – for ropes, marine plywood, pulleys, woodwork tools and elasticated rope.

www.communityplaythings.co.uk – for wooden blocks (various sizes) and storage units.

www.costco.co.uk – for heavy duty tarpaulins and shelving.

www.cosydirect.com – for open-ended resources at reasonable prices.

www.ikea.co.uk – for storage units, canopies and children's furniture.

www.impbins.com – for salt bins.

www.olympicgymnasium.com – for A-Frames and ladders, etc. Look in the "nursery" section.

www.pvc-strip.co.uk – for plastic strips to hang in doorways.

www.shedstore.co.uk – for sheds (Model: Larchlap Overlap Maxi Wallstore 63 is useful for storing large wooden blocks).

www.earlyexcellence.com – for open shelving in particular.

www.filplastic.co.uk – for shopping baskets.

Bibliography

Athey, C. 1990. *Extending Thought in Young Children: A Parent–Teacher Partnership*. Paul Chapman Publishing Ltd. London.

Bilton, H. 2010. *Outdoor Learning in the Early Years*. Routledge. Oxfordshire.

Bowlby, J. 1997. *Attachment and Loss*. Pimlico. London.

Brooker, L. 2002. *Starting School*. Oxford University Press. Oxford.

Bruce, T. 2005. *Early Childhood Education*. 3rd Edition. Hodder and Stoughton. London.

Bruce, T. 2001. *Learning Through Play: Babies, Toddlers and the Foundation Years*. Hodder Arnold. London.

Dyer, W. 2007. *Mercury's Child*. Booklocker.com, Inc. for Colly and Sons UK.

Ephgrave, A. 2012. *The Reception Year in Action*. 2nd Edition. Routledge. Oxfordshire.

Ephgrave, A. 2015. *The Nursery Year in Action*. Routledge. Oxfordshire.

Ephgrave, A. 2017. *Year One in Action*. Routledge. Oxfordshire.

Fisher, J. 2002. *Starting From The Child*. 2nd Edition. Open University Press. Maidenhead.

Gerhardt, S. 2004. *Why Love Matters*. Routledge. Hove.

Gray, P. 2013. *Free to Learn*. Basic Books. New York.

Greenfield, S. 2014. *Mind Change*. Rider. London.

Gussin-Paley, V. 1991. *The Boy Who Would Be A Helicopter*. Harvard University Press. Massachusetts.

Isaacs, S. 1966. *Intellectual Growth in Young Children*. Shockern Books. New York.

Isaacs, S. 1929. *The Nursery Years*. Routledge & Kegan Paul. London.

Laevers, F. 1994. *Five Levels of Well-Being*. Leuven University Press.

Legerstee, M., Haley, D. & Bornstein, M. 2013. *The Infant Mind*. The Guilford Press. New York.

Nutbrown, C. 2006. *Threads of Thinking*. 3rd Edition. Sage. London.

Pellegrini, A. D. 2011. *The Oxford Handbook of the Development of Play*. Oxford University Press. Oxford.

Read, V. & Hughes, A. 2009. *Developing Attachment in Early Years Settings*. David Fulton Publishers. Oxfordshire.

Robinson, D. & Groves, J. 2002. *Introducing Bertrand Russell*. Icon Books. Cambridge.

Robinson, K. & Aronica, L. 2015. *Creative Schools*. Viking Penguin. USA.

Russell, D. 1932. *In Defence of Children*. Hamish Hamilton. London.

Solly, K. 2014. *Risk, Challenge and Adventure in the Early Years*. Routledge. Oxfordshire.

Vygotsky, L. S. 1987. *Mind in Society*. Harvard University Press. USA.

Whalley, M. 2007. *Involving Parents in their Children's Learning*. 2nd Edition. Paul Chapman Publishing. London.

Index